racing
systems
with the
pocket calculator

racing
systems
with the
pocket calculator

john white

foulsham
LONDON • NEW YORK • TORONTO • SYDNEY

foulsham

The Publishing House, Bennetts Close, Cippenham, Berkshire, SL1 5AP, England

ISBN 0-572-02691-9

Printed in Great Britain by St. Edmundsbury Press, Bury St. Edmunds, Suffolk

*For my family, for Jo
and for all my students*

ACKNOWLEDGEMENTS

My debts to my typist, to Derrick Payne for first getting me 'button-pressing' and to the producers of the racing pages of daily and racing newspapers are all considerable.

ABOUT THE AUTHOR

In 1990, John White was voted Magazine Sportswriter of the Year. A past contributor to the *Sporting Life Weekender*, the *Observer* Colour Supplement, *Competition Rider*, *Royalty Monthly*, *The Lady*, *The Irish Field*, *Equestrian World*, *Mensa Magazine*, *Writer's Monthly*, the *Sunday Telegraph*, *The Betting Man's Contact* and to *Racing Monthly* and *Turf and Track* as a systems expert, he has already published a predecessor to this book, as well as *First Past the Post, Dark Secrets of the Turf* and *More Dark Secrets of the Turf* – all compendia of strategies for making racing far more profitable and enjoyable – in addition to a complete encyclopedia of racing for Harper Collins.

CONTENTS

INTRODUCTION

As Mark Twain so wisely said, 'it is the difference of opinion that makes horse racing' and yet, because the initial opinion of many a backer is abandoned, winners are regularly missed. Self-recrimination is the inevitable upshot, as the 'Sport of Kings', and of so many of their subjects, again proves too stern a test of character. Significantly though, those who fail the test, like anglers describing 'the one that got away', often report how it would have been otherwise had they followed their initial inclinations.

The problem here lies not with Lady Luck but with our fickle human nature. 'Striving to better, oft we mar what's well' since, out of greed, or in the emotional heat of the betting moment, we behave in ways we later rue as near lunatic betrayals of our past convictions or lessons previously learnt the hard way.

One explanation for the changes of heart and mind to which backers prove so susceptible is that the betting forecast and, to an even greater extent, the actual course betting, do a great deal to distort the, initially, quite dispassionate assessments of horses' winning chances that backers may engage in as they process the many non-financial, usually form-based, variables that so crucially influence the results of races.

For example, the lemming-like behaviour of many racegoers and betting shop habitués in abandoning their initial fancies selected on rational criteria, for 'false' favourites or 'springers' whose opening prices are massively trimmed, is one major reason why, in bookmakers' parlance, the horse leading the market is known as the 'jolly' and why those who blindly follow the money find the road to fortune is made up of losing distances.

Fortunately though, thanks to the pocket calculator – today so widely available and used in a whole host of general, educational, scientific and commercial applications – the backer can acquire a 'minder' to ensure that he or she does not, through sheer fickleness and lack of faith in initial form assessments, become his or her own worst enemy and the friend of bookmakers.

CHAPTER 1

CALCULATING THE RACES
ON WHICH TO WORK

In its capacity as the 'minder' of the backer, the pocket calculator should not be asked to offer protection against the dangers of operating in the high-risk area that a race with a large field represents. Thus, on any racing day, the backer should first discount all races which have more than ten runners, not just because bookmakers are more likely to offer overall value for money when they are offering odds against a small number of runners, but because any effect the draw may have and the risk of interference in running are both likely to be reduced if a small field faces the starter.

The backer should start by calculating which race with a smallish field is the one least likely to produce a freak result. This, as long experience has shown, is often the race which carries the greatest prize money – perhaps one of the many 'pattern' or 'listed' races that are staged each season, which tend to be won by horses with obvious claims on form and time. Alternatively, there may be a less prestigious non-handicap or rich handicap which has not attracted a large field.

Value of race to its winner in £ (its added or penalty value)	Rating to be entered into memory for race with 10 or fewer runners
100,001 or more	18
50,001 – 100,000	17
40,001 – 50,000	16
30,001 – 40,000	15
20,001 – 30,000	14
15,001 – 20,000	13
12,501 – 15,000	12
10,001 – 12,500	11
9,001 – 10,000	10
8,001 – 9,000	9
7,001 – 8,000	8
6,001 – 7,000	7
5,001 – 6,000	6
4,001 – 5,000	5
3,001 – 4,000	4
2,001 – 3,000	3
1,001 – 2,000	2
less than 1,000	1

Figure 1

In practice, after eliminating all other races, the backer should give each of the day's surviving races with ten or fewer runners a rating based on its class, as reflected by the prize money the winner will collect, i.e. the race's penalty value as indicated in newspapers. In fact, this class rating, as indicated in the right hand column in Figure 1, is the first number that should be keyed into the calculator's memory. If this facility is not available on the particular machine being used it should be entered for later augmentation.

An example taken from a prestigious recently contested race – the 2000 King George VI and Queen Elizabeth Diamond Stakes – should make what is involved crystal clear.

3.50 KING GEORGE VI & QUEEN ELIZABETH DIAMOND STAKES (GR1) (A); £435,000; 1m 4f   (7 runners)

Figure 2

Since the winner of this race was due to collect £435,000 it received a class rating, based on the prize money, of 18 points, as can be seen from Figure 1.

As is suggested by the frequently voiced belief that in some years Epsom Derby fields are 'sub-standard', sizeable prize money alone is no guarantee that races will actually be contested by top-class performers, which tend to run up to their best form more often and provide win-and-place dividends more frequently than do more moderate racehorses. Thus, the backer should key into the calculator's memory a second numerical assessment of the actual ability of those that are due to take part in the race under consideration.

Average of (a) average of Topspeed's three highest ratings and (b) that of Postmark's equivalent figures	Points to be awarded
141+	18
136 – 140	17
130 – 135	16
124 – 129	15
118 – 123	14
112 – 117	13
106 – 111	12

100 – 105	11
94 – 99	10
88 – 93	9
82 – 87	8
76 – 81	7
70 – 75	6
64 – 69	5
58 – 63	4
52 – 57	3
46 – 51	2
41 – 45	1

Figure 3

In doing this, the backer should enlist the help of two private handicappers. These are 'Postmark' and 'Topspeed' of the *Racing Post*. Postmark assesses horses' form and Topspeed their time performances. They both, most conveniently, work to the same scales – 0–140, (0–10st) for flat racing and 0–175, (0–12st 7 lb) for jumping races – as the official Jockey Club handicapper and thus both usefully allow their ratings to be directly compared with the official 'marks'.

All one has to do is work out the following two calculations:

a) the average of Postmark's top three ratings for the race

b) the average of the three highest ratings that Topspeed provides.

All that now remains is to calculate the average of (a) and (b). The resultant figure is then awarded points according to its size, as shown in Figure 3.

This may sound a little complicated but is actually quite straightforward, as should emerge from the following worked example covering the previously featured seven-runner King George VI and Queen Elizabeth Diamond Stakes, run at Ascot in July 2000. This was assessed by Postmark and Topspeed as shown in Figures 4 and 5.

ADJUSTED OFFICIAL RATING	**3.50**		POSTMARK LATEST / BEST / ADJ		
124 **Beat All**	. . . .	.9-7	126	126	**126**
129 **Daliapour**	. . . .	.9-7	131	131	**131**
131 **Fantastic Light**	. . . .	.9-7	124	133	**133**
131 **Fruits of Love**	. . . .	.9-7	129	129	**134**
142 **Montjeu**	. . . .	.9-7	134 ◀	144 ◀	**144 ◀**
131 **Shiva**	. . . .	.9-4	131	139	**133**
118 **Raypour**	. . . .	.8-9	111	111	**111**

Figure 4

3.50		Topspeed Ratings		
	LATEST	BEST		ADJUSTED
Beat All	118	118-Jul 17 Ayr	10.0gf	118
Daliapour	119	119-Jun 09 Epsm	12.0gs	**125**
Fantastic Light	111	118-Jun 09 Epsm	12.0gs	120
Fruits Of Love	**121**	**121**-Jun 23 Asct	12.0gf	121
Montjeu	–			121
Shiva	119	120-May 30 Sand	10.0hy	122
Raypour	119	119-Jul 02 Curr	12.0y	119

Figure 5

Next the average of Postmark's top three ratings listed in the 'adjusted' column was taken, i.e. of 144, 134 and 133 = 411 ÷ 3 = 137. When applied to Topspeed's top three ratings, this same averaging process gave a figure of 123 (i.e. 368 ÷ 3). The average of these two average figures, representing class on form and class on time respectively, worked out at – to the nearest whole number – 130. This, according to Figure 3, gave a score of 16 that was then added into the calculator's memory.

Having thus thoroughly rated the class of a qualifying non-handicap according to both the prize money it carries and the calibre of its contestants as rated by a private handicapper working on past form and another on previous performances against the clock, it is time to assess the race according to a third criterion. This involves the distance over which it is to be staged, for the simple reason that a horse which a stop-watch holder and a form assessor feel has a sizeable pull over its rivals will be able to make this advantage really tell if it is due to race over a considerable distance of ground.

Thus, a rating is next added into the calculator's memory to reflect the number of furlongs the race under consideration involves. The more furlongs covered, the greater is the rating score that is keyed in, as can be seen in Figure 6.

Distance of race in furlongs	Points to be awarded
22	18
21	17
20	16
19	15
18	14
17	13
16	12
15	11
14	10
13	9
12	8
11	7
10	6
9	5
8	4
7	3
6	2
5	1

Figure 6

The fourth and final stage of allotting a 'suitability for investment' score to a qualifying race involves an assessment of how competitive or otherwise it seems. The latter state is obviously what the backer should seek to capitalise upon and, in general, its possible presence will be signalled if the race under consideration can be seen to have attracted a small number of runners.

In the belief that the racing adage 'the bigger the field, the bigger the certainty' is illogical, your chosen race is given a score according to Figure 7.

Number of runners	Points to be awarded
2	18
3	16
4	14
5	12
6	10
7	8
8	6
9	4
10	2

Figure 7

Thus, the previously featured King George VI and Queen Elizabeth Diamond Stakes, having attracted seven runners, was given a rating of 8 which was the final figure that was added into the memory of the calculator. Interestingly, as a true 'punter's friend' it pointed to this top-class Group I, all-aged, one-and-a-half mile championship race as being the one most suitable for finding winners by calculator on Saturday 29 July 2000.

This race had, after all, been credited with a high final score of 50, i.e. 18 for its prize money plus 16 (for the class of its highest-rated contenders) plus 8 (for its distance) plus a final 8 (for its small, seven runner field).

Those backers who cannot gain access to the specialist racing daily, the *Racing Post*, should add in three of the four figures discussed above into the calculator's memory. These are the first (relating to prize money), the third (relating to race distance) and the fourth (relating to the number of runners due to compete) – all of which are shown in any daily or evening newspaper that has a racing page.

3.50 **KING GEORGE VI & QUEEN ELIZABETH DIAMOND STAKES (GR1) (A); £435,000; 1m 4f   (7 runners)**

Figure 8

As can be seen (above), such a publication would have given sufficient information for the featured King George VI and Queen Elizabeth Diamond Stakes to have been given an 'investment suitability' rating of 34, i.e. 18 for prize money + 8 for race distance + 8 for attracting seven runners.

Naturally, assessments relating to the suitability for investment purposes of hurdle races and steeplechases can just as readily be made according to the four criteria already described. This will be possible if the following table is used. This reflects the fact that races staged under National Hunt rules are generally worth less to their winners than is the case on the flat, take place over longer distances and feature horses that Postmark and Topspeed assess, not from 0–140 (0–10st), but from 0–175 (0–12st 7lb).

Example: Were (implausibly) a jumping race, worth over £50,000 to its winner, to involve just two runners whose form and time ratings as given in the *Racing Post* averaged out at over 170 and, were it to be run over more than four miles, it would be given an unassailable 'investment suitability' rating of 4 × 18 = 72.

POINTS TABLE FOR NATIONAL HUNT SELECTIONS

Points for each Factor	Factor A: Prize Money to Winner £	Factor B: Average of Averages of Postmark and Topspeed	Factor C: Race Distance in Furlongs	Factor D: No. of Runners
18	over 50,000	171+	over 32	2
17	40,001 – 50,000	161–170	32	
16	30,001 – 40,000	151–160	31	3
15	20,001 – 30,000	141–150	30	
14	15,001 – 20,000	131–140	29	4
13	12,501 – 15,000	121–130	28	
12	10,001 – 12,500	111–120	27	5
11	8,001 – 10,000	101–110	26	
10	7,001 – 8,000	91–100	25	6
9	6,001 – 7,000	81–90	24	
8	5,001 – 6,000	71–80	23	7
7	4,001 – 5,000	61–70	22	
6	3,001 – 4,000	51–60	21	8
5	2,501 – 3,000	41–50	20	
4	2,001 – 2,500	31–40	19	9
3	1,501 – 2,000	21–30	18	
2	1,001 – 1,500	11–20	17	10
1	less than 1,000	1–10	16	

Figure 9

CHAPTER 2

CALCULATING WHAT TO BET BY COMPUTING HORSE RACE FORM

H aving determined, on the basis of its highest points score – memory-added into the calculator from the tables in Chapter 1 – which Flat or National Hunt race should ease the crucial task of finding winners, it is time to perform this with a calculator.

The starting point for this process consists of making additions to the ratings of Postmark and Topspeed, already discussed, which are compatible in the sense that they both feature the same scales of 0–140 (0–10st) for flat racing or, for jumping races, of 0–175 (0–12st 7lb). These form and time figures are added together and then averaged by being halved; the resultant figure is the first that is entered into the calculator's memory. Hereafter, most reassuringly, this generally under-used device really comes into its own as it 'forces' the backer to take account of several variables that long experience and also the advice of private handicappers suggest so often exert a major influence on the outcomes of many races.

Whatever calculator is used, it will tackle the task of finding winners in a manner that is far more scientific, objective and relevant than the *modus operandi* of the most disciplined and unemotional of horse players. Such a thought is most encouraging since the ability of 50 such individuals to behave like computers in processing a mass of data in a completely interactive way led two researchers from Cornell University to class their decision-making as comparable to that of brain surgeons!

Understandably, then, consideration of what variables to take account of in assessing horses' winning prospects has involved what these Cornell researchers identified as the key elements in the thinking of these 50 'super punters'. Significantly, and most reassuringly, these in fact correspond with many of the 'race-day factors' which some compilers of newspaper private handicaps so regret they have been unable to consider 24 hours before racing that they actually refer to them in caveats they append to their ratings. Of these 'race-day' factors, fitness is so crucial that Peter Braddock makes it a cornerstone of the selection method he recommends in his *Complete Guide to Horse Race Selection and Betting* (Longmans, 1987).

Moreover, in one of the best general guides to racing ever published, Kenneth Stewart's *A Background to Racing*, designations such as 'fit to run', 'fit to run a good race' and 'fit to win' were used to differentiate between runners that, through recent outings on the racecourse, or lack of these, could, or could not, be expected to run up to their previous form. To take account of the fitness of a runner, a certain number of points, as shown in the following table, is added to the average (i.e. the half) of the sum that results when its form rating is added to its time one.

Days since horse last ran on a racecourse	Number of points to be awarded
1 – 2	10
3 – 6	9
7 – 10	8
11 – 14	7
15 – 21	6
22 – 28	5
29 – 35	4
36 – 50	3
51 – 100	2
101+	1

Figure 10

The figures that result from this amendment process are then adjusted to take account of the possible suitability to the horse concerned of some factors which Postmark and Topspeed do not include in their calculations, but which are revealed elsewhere in the *Racing Post*'s extensive form coverage. This involves further bonus points being added to a runner's rating as indicated in the course, distance and going table (Figure 11).

Conditions	Points to be awarded
Runner has gained more than one previous win over course and distance and has won on prevailing going	8
Runner has gained one previous course and distance win and won on prevailing going or, alternatively, has gained a course victory over a different distance, a distance win elsewhere and also won on prevailing going	6
Runner has gained a course win over a different distance and has scored on prevailing going, or won over a different distance on the course and going, or has gained a course and distance victory on different going	4
Runner has merely a course win, or a distance win on another course, or a past win over a different distance on the prevailing going	2

Figure 11

Whatever horse emerges as top-rated after this second, rather sophisticated, amendment to averaged-out amalgamations of 'raw' form and time ratings is definitely one that the backer who wisely uses a pocket calculator to work on data given in the *Racing Post* should seriously consider.

To make matters plain, the following is a worked example showing exactly what happened when the ratings that Postmark and Topspeed provided for this newspaper as part of its coverage of the already featured King George VI Stakes were added, averaged and then adjusted to take account of race fitness and the suitability to the horses concerned of the Ascot course, the 12-furlong race distance and the good-to-firm going that prevailed on the royal course on 29 July 2000.

For convenience the ratings accorded the 'King George' field by Postmark and Topspeed are again shown in Figures 12 and 13.

ADJUSTED OFFICIAL RATING	**3.50**		POSTMARK LATEST / BEST / ADJ		
124 **Beat All**	....	9-7	126	126	**126**
129 **Daliapour**	....	9-7	131	131	**131**
131 **Fantastic Light**	....	9-7	124	133	**133**
131 **Fruits of Love**	....	9-7	129	129	**134**
142 **Montjeu**	....	9-7	134 ◄	144 ◄	**144 ◄**
131 **Shiva**	....	9-4	131	139	**133**
118 **Raypour**	....	8-9	111	111	**111**

Figure 12

3.50		Topspeed Ratings		
	LATEST	BEST		ADJUSTED
Beat All	118	118-Jul 17 Ayr	10.0gf	118
Daliapour	119	119-Jun 09 Epsm	12.0gs	**125**
Fantastic Light	111	118-Jun 09 Epsm	12.0gs	120
Fruits Of Love	**121**	**121**-Jun 23 Asct	12.0gf	121
Montjeu	−			121
Shiva	119	120-May 30 Sand	10.0hy	122
Raypour	119	119-Jul 02 Curr	12.0y	119

Figure 13

When combined, Postmark's and Topspeed's figures became:

Beat All	244
Daliapour	256
Fantastic Light	253
Fruits of Love	N/R
Montjeu	265
Shiva	255
Raypour	230

When averaged out (i.e. divided by two) these ratings changed to:

Beat All	122
Daliapour	128
Fantastic Light	126
Montjeu	132
Shiva	127
Raypour	115

The above ratings formed the starting point for calculations involving every form and time-rated runner for the 'King George' and, as such, were entered into the calculator's memory. Then, the fitness-points table (*see* Figure 10) was consulted and further points keyed in for each runner, to reflect its race fitness, or lack of this (*see also* Figure 14). This changed the ratings to:

Beat All	$122 + 7 = 129$
Daliapour	$128 + 3 = 131$
Fantastic Light	$126 + 6 = 132$
Montjeu	$132 + 5 = 137$
Shiva	$127 + 6 = 133$
Raypour	$115 + 5 = 120$

Next the course, distance and going table (*see* Figure 11) was consulted. To allow this to take account of the last-mentioned of these factors – the good-to-firm ground to be found at Ascot on 29 July 2000 – the runners' form summaries, as given in the *Racing Post* (*see* Figure 15) were studied. After points from the course, distance and going table (Figure 11) had, where appropriate, been memory-added to each runner's score, the following figures appeared on the calculator's display panel:

Beat All	129 (from 129 + 0)
Daliapour	135 (from 131 + 4)
Fantastic Light	134 (from 132 + 2)
Montjeu	139 (from 137 + 2)
Shiva	133 (from 133 + 0)
Raypour	120 (from 120 + 0)

Thus, Montjeu finally emerged with a rating of 139 as the clear top-rated selection. In the event his superiority was widely recognised and his owner landed a bet of £90,000 that he would win his race. This he did contemptuously (from Fantastic Light and the slightly disappointing Daliapour) at 1–3, to the delight of the many professional backers present at Ascot who were only too happy to take this price on what the calculator suggested was a certainty.

Going: GOOD TO FIRM (Good in places)

3.50	*King George VI and Queen*	**BBC1**
RACE 4	*Elizabeth Diamond Stakes (Class A)*	
	(Group 1)	
	Winner £435,000	**1m4f**

£750000 guaranteed **For** 3yo+ **Weights** 3yo colts and geldings 8st 9lb; fillies 8st 6lb; 470= colts and geldings 9st 7lb; fillies 9st 4lb (southern hemisphere allowance: 3yo 6lb; 4yo 2lb) **Weight for age** 3 from 4yo+ 12lb **Entries** 40 pay £2200 **1st Forfeit** 17 pay £2600 **Confirmed** 11 pay £1600 **Penalty value 1st** £435,000 **2nd** £165,000 **3rd** £82,500 **4th** £37,500 **5th** £18,750 **6th** £11,250

134-432 **1** (4)	**BEAT ALL** (USA) [12] *b c Dynaformer-Spirited Missus* **Sir Michael Stoute** Saeed Suhail	4 9-7 **K Darley** (126)	
2228-11 **2** (3)	**DALIAPOUR** (IRE) [50] *b c Sadler's Wells-Dalara* **Sir Michael Stoute** H H Aga Khan	4 9-7 **J P Murtagh** (131)	
110-125 **3** (7)	**FANTASTIC LIGHT** (USA) [21] *b c Rahy-Jood* **Saeed Bin Suroor** Godolphin	4 9-7 **J Reid** (133)	
61329-1 **4** (2)	**FRUITS OF LOVE** (USA) [36] *b h Hansel-Vallee Secrete* **M Johnston** M Doyle	v5 9-7 **NON-RUNNER** (134)	
1114-11 **5** (5)	**MONTJEU** (IRE) [27] *b c Sadler's Wells-Floripedes* **J E Hammond (FR)** M Tabor	4 9-7 **M J Kinane** (144)	
172-713 **6** (1)	**SHIVA** (JPN) [21] *ch m Hector Protector-Lingerie* **H R A Cecil** Niarchos Family	5 9-4 **T Quinn** (133)	
121-212 **7** (8)	**AIR SHAKUR** (JPN) [62] *b c Sunday Silence-I Dreamed A Dream* **Hideyuki Mori (JPN)** Lucky Field Co Ltd	3 8-9 **Y Take**	
2-22624 **8** (6)	**RAYPOUR** (IRE) [27] *ch c Barathea-Rayseka* **John M Oxx (IRE)** H H Aga Khan	3 8-9 **J Fortune** (111)	

● **SHIVA** runs only if sufficient rain, states trainer

1999 (8 ran) **Daylami** (8) Saeed Bin Suroor 5 9-7 3/1   L Dettori PM133

BETTING FORECAST: 1-2 Montjeu, 4 Daliapour, 9 Fantastic Light, 10 Air Shakur, Shiva, 25 Beat All, 66 Raypour.

Figure 14

Beat All   9-7

4-y-o *b c Dynaformer - Spirited Missus (Distinctive)*
Sir Michael Stoute   K Darley

Placings: 21/134-432   **Draw:** 4

OR117	Starts	1st	2nd	3rd	Win & Pl
All Flat races 8		2	2	2	**£193,742**

4/99	NmkJ	1m2f A List 3yo good £12,842	
9/98	NmkJ	7f D Mdn 2yo gd-sft £3,014	

Total win prize-money £15,856

Going (GF): 0-2-3   **Course:** 0-0-1   **Distance:** 0-1-2

Fantastic Light   9-7

4-y-o *b c Rahy-Jood (Nijinksy)*
Saeed Bin Suroor   J Reid

Placings: 113/1423110-125   **Draw:** 7

OR124	Starts	1st	2nd	3rd	Win & Pl
All Flat races 13		6	2	2	**£992,479**

3/00	Ndas	1m4f Gp3 good £731,707
9/99	Newb	1m3f A List gd-sft £28,750
8/99	York	1m4f A Gp2 3yo good £57,000
4/98	Sand	1m2f A Gp3 3yo soft £39,870
8/98	Sand	1m C 2yo gd-fm £4,279
8/98	Sand	7f D 2yo good £4,104

Total win prize-money £865,710

Going (GF): 1-2-4   **Course:** 0-1-1   **Distance:** 2-0-4

Shiva   9-4

5-y-o *ch m Hector Protector-Lingerie (Shirley Heights)*
H R A Cecil   T Quinn

Placings: 1/1172-713   **Draw:** 1

OR121	Starts	1st	2nd	3rd	Win & Pl
All Flat races 8		4	1	1	**£235,280**

5/00	Sand	1m2f A Gp3 heavy £24,000
5/99	Curr	1m2½f Gp1 good £62,000
4/99	NmkJ	1m½f A Gp3 good £20,000
5/98	Kemp	1m1f D Mdn 3yo good £3,680

Total win prize-money £109,680

Going (GF): 0-1-1   **Course:** 0-0-1   **Distance:** 0-0-0

Figure 15(a)

Daliapour   9-7

4-y-o *b c Sadler's Wells-Dalara (Doyoun)*
Sir Michael Stoute   J P Murtagh
Placings: 6131/12228-11   **Draw:** 3

OR122

		Starts	1st	2nd	3rd	Win & Pl
All Flat races	11		5	3	1	**£602,539**
6/00	Epsm	1m4f A Gp 1 gd-sft £150,000				
5/00	Ches	1m5½f A Gp 3 good £36,000				
4/99	Epsm	1m2f B 3yo soft £8,760				
10/98	Asct	1m A List 2yo soft £12,663				
8/98	Chep	1m D Mdn 2yo gd-fm £3,388				

Total win prize-money £210,811

Going (GF): 1-1-3   **Course:** 1-0-2   **Distance:** 1-2-4

Montjeu   9-7

4-y-o *b c Sadler's Wells-Floripedes (Top Ville)*
J E Hammond (FR)   M J Kinane
Placings: 11/1211114-11   **Draw:** 5

OR135

		Starts	1st	2nd	3rd	Win & Pl
All Flat races	11		9	1	–	**£1,704,572**
7/00	StCl	1m4f Gp1 good £115,274				
5/00	Curr	1m2½f Gp 1 gd-yld £63,000				
10/99	Lonc	1m4f Gp1 heavy £538,213				
9/99	Lonc	1m4f Gp2 3yo good £43,057				
6/99	Curr	1m4f Gp1 3yo good £440,555				
4/99	Lonc	1m2¼f Gp2 3yo holding £32,293				
10/98	Lonc	1m1f List 2yo heavy £14,141				
9/98	Chan	1m 2yo good £8,081				

Total win prize-money £1,523,721

Going (GF): 0-0-0   **Course:** 0-0-0   **Distance:** 5-0-6

Raypour   8-9

3-y-o *ch c Barathea (8.2f)-Rayseka (Dancing Brave)*
John M Oxx (IRE)   J Fortune
Placings: 042-22624   **Draw:** 6

OR111

		Starts	1st	2nd	3rd	Win & Pl
All Flat races	8		–	4	–	**£33,120**

Going (GF): 0-0-0   **Course:** 0-0-0 ....**Distance:** 0-1-2

Figure 15(b)

We will now look at an even more advanced method of forecasting by calculator and, as is only to be expected, this again involves data provided in the specialist racing daily, the *Racing Post*.

2311P3-433 ONLY TROUBLE (9-11-8) (T J Houlbrooke) b or br m Trasi's Son - Kadella by Kadir Cup **1988-89, 21/2m ch heavy (Haydock), 3m ch heavy (Chepstow) £9,987 (-).**
LWR (89+90): 2m4f ch **96** (Dis)   TR: **106**

Jan 8, Wolverhampton, 3 m 1f h'cap chase (0-135), good, £3,054: 1 Rymer King (8-10-11), 2 A Boy Named Sioux (10-10-4), 3 ONLY TROUBLE (9-10-5, H Davies), **always prominent, led tenth till headed 15th, ridden two out, kept on one pace.** (5 to 1 op 7 to 1 tchd 8 to 1); 9 Ran. 1l, 8l, 3l, 20l, 5l. 6m 23.60s (a 8.60s).
RACECHECK: Wins 0, pl 2, unpl 4.

Dec 23, Chepstow, 2½m h'cap chase (0-125), soft, £3,039: 1 The Legget (6-10-7), 2 Wally Wombat (11-10-1), 3 ONLY TROUBLE (8-10-11, B Powell), **chased leaders until lost place halfway, stayed on again from two out.** (4 to 1 op 5 to 1 tchd 6 to 1); 13 Ran. 12l, 7l, 4l, 3l, 6l, 5m 16.50s (a 26.50s). SR: 24/6/9/-/-/1.
RACECHECK: Wins 5, pl 6, unpl 13.

Dec 4, Worcester, 2½m h'cap chase (0-125), good to firm, £3,392: 1 Toby Tobias (7-12-0), 2 Arctic Cavalier (7-10-7), 3 Pride Hill (7-10-2,5*), 4 ONLY TROUBLE (8-10-10, H Davies), **pressed leader until weakened approaching 12th.** (11 to 1 op 10 to 1 tchd 12 to 1); 11 Ran. 8l, 2l, 25l, 5l, 8l, cht-hd, 25l. 5m 17.10s (a21.10s).
RACECHECK: Wins 3, pl 9, unpl 15.

Figure 16

As class is such a crucial factor, it again plays a prominent part in calculations but, on this occasion, it is assessed in Step 1 by dividing the amount of money that a horse has won in its racing career by the number of victories it has registered in this time.

If, for example, the first *Racing Post* figure indicating such prize money (not the bracketed second figure which, where applicable, relates to winning sums gained in the current season only) was £9987, as in the example in Figure 16, and the number of individual victories the horse has gained in its career (which can be gleaned from the details of these shown in its form summary) was seen to be two, a simple division sum would reveal that its average 'pick up' as a past winner has been £4993.

The backer should delete the last two digits of this average prize money figure after rounding to the nearest £100, as in the above example, where the figure in question (from £4993) would be 50.

This figure should be keyed into the calculator prior to pressing its + key.

In Step 2 all the entries appearing in a horse's form line should be given points according to where the horse finished in recent contests.

10 points should be given for each current season win.
 8 points should be given for each current season second.
 6 points should be given for each current season third.
 4 points should be given for each current season fourth.
 2 points should be given for each current season fifth.
 0 points should be given for each current season place worse
         than fifth.

If a horse's current season form line consists of more than two entries, it is not necessary to take account of any of its previous seasons' form figures that may be included in this form line. If this involves only one or two runs in the current season or no outings at all in this season, calculations should be based on a horse's last three outings irrespective of season. Moreover, if the backer sees the symbols P, R, B or F, which indicate that a runner has been pulled up, has refused to jump a fence, has been brought down or has fallen, these should be regarded as 'unplaced' runs.

Thus, if a runner's current season form line reads as 433, as in the case of Only Trouble, it would receive a seasonal finishing position score of 16 (*see* Figure 16). This score should be divided by its total number of outings – three. The resultant figure (rounded up or down to the nearest whole number where necessary) should be keyed into the calculator, prior to pressing its – key. In the above example, the figure so entered was 5.33, i.e. 5.

Step 3 takes into account is the horse's position last time out and this means that a previous winner should be given a score of 1, a second last time out 2, a third 3, a fourth 4 and so on. Conveniently, the last right-hand entry in each runner's form line will show the figure required which should be noted as the third to be entered into the calculator before, on this occasion, pressing the = key and then the × key.

In Only Trouble's case, the figure 3 indicated its position last time out and this was keyed in, the = key pressed and the × button depressed.

Finally, in Steps 4 and 5 there comes a sophisticated set of computations that allow full statistical advantage to be taken of a feature the *Racing Post* took over from the now defunct *Sporting Life*. This is 'Racecheck' which indicates how many winners (WINS), placed horses (PL) and unplaced horses (UNPL) have come out of a particular past race since it was run (*see* Figure 16).

The example of this Racecheck feature (shown above in Figure 16) reveals that on two recent occasions the mare Only Trouble was crucially placed in races whose 'productivity' as regards subsequent winners, placed horses and unplaced ones has already been calculated by the *Racing Post*.

What the backer should do is first discount any Racecheck races, such as Only Trouble's on 4 December, in which a placing in the first three was not achieved, before computing the 'productivity' of all its other recent races in which it did 'make the frame'.

In Step 4 the grand total of all wins and places shown in the appropriate Racecheck entries is first entered into the calculator. In Only Trouble's case, her races on 23 December (in which she came third) and on 8 January (in which she came third again) between them produced 13 as the first figure so entered to assess the worth of this runner's recent form (i.e. 5 wins and 6 places, plus 0 wins and 2 places). Then the calculator's = key was pressed.

In Step 5, to the 13 calculated in Step 4 is added 17, representing the number of unplaced runs by horses in the two races (i.e. 13 from 23 December plus 4 from 8 January), to give a total of 30. After the calculator's × key was operated, the number 100 keyed in and the ÷ sign engaged this figure of 30 was entered, before the = key was pressed and finally the √ key engaged. This gave a final rating of 47.47.

As what was needed to arrive at this may sound a little bewildering and complicated, Figure 17 simplifies and summarises what is required in step-by-step format and applies it to Only Trouble's past form.

Step 1 (**Rating prize money**)	Enter first two digits of 'average prize money' figure (50 for Only Trouble).
Step 2 (**Rating the form line**)	Press + key Enter form line rating figure (5 for Only Trouble).
Step 3 (**Rating the latest run**)	Press – key Enter last figure shown in current season's form line (3 for Only Trouble). Press = key.
Step 4 (**First stage of rating 'worth' of recent placed form**)	Press × key Enter 'Racecheck' places figure (13 for Only Trouble) Press = key.
Step 5 (**Second stage of rating 'worth' of recent placed form**)	Press × key Enter 100 Enter ÷ key Enter Racecheck 'total runs' figure (30 for Only Trouble)
Step 6 (**Arriving at a final rating**)	Press = key Press √ key for horse's final rating (for Only Trouble = 47.47)

Figure 17

As the above amounts to a fairly complex selection procedure, the following is a worked example of an actual race, assessed according to its principles. The race was a novices' chase run at Ayr and, of the 20 runners this involved, only seven had Racecheck entries as part of their past form. These are shown in Figure 18.

ASTRE RADIEUX (FR)   5-10-2
/4423-4450221221   **S Mellor**
b g Gay Mecene (USA) - Divine Etoile (USA)
by Nijinsky (CAN)
  1989-90 (Jan) 2½m ch good/soft (Warwick)
nov; **(Mar)** 2m ch good (Hexham) nov. £5,033.
LWR (89+90): -   TR: **95**
  March 15, Hexham, 2m nov chase, good, £2,247:
1 ASTRE RADIEUX (5-11-3, Mr D Gray), **jumped
boldly, made most, clear after three out, readily**
(4/6 op 8/11) 2 Contact Kelvin (8-11-4), 3 Majestic
Ring (8-11-4); 13 Ran. 5l, 25l, 3l, 15l, 2l, sht-hd. 4m
5.30s (a 7.30s). SR: 24/20/-/-/-/-.
RACECHECK: Wins 2, pl 4, unpl 11.
  March 10, Chepstow. See ROMANY KING
  March 2, Haydock, 2m Hcp chase (0-125, 119),
heavy, £3,542: 1 The Leggett (7-11-1, inc 4lb ex),
2 ASTRE RADIEUX (5-10-0, **94**, S Cowley),
**always handy, led or disputed lead from six out,
kept on same pace run-in.** (100/30 op 7/2 tchd 4/1
and 3/1) 3 General Chandos (9-11-10); 4 Ran. 1½l,
30l. 4m 26.80s (a 24.80s). SR: 49/22/16.
RACECHECK: Wins 2, pl 3, unpl 3.

TARTAN TEMPEST   7-11-2
0554510F16-B414U2   **G W Richards**
br g Crozier - Frello by Bargello **1988-89** 2¾m h
heavy (Ayr); 2½m h soft (Carlisle)
  1989-90 (Dec) 3m ch good/soft (Hexham)
nov. £4,504 (£2,120).
LWR (89+90): 93 (Nk)   TR: **99**
  March 9, Carlisle, 3m nov chase, soft, £2,177:
1 Super Fountain (7-10-5), 2 TARTAN TEMPEST
(7-11-3, N Doughty), **patiently ridden, joined
leaders on bit four out, led after last, soon
headed and not quicken.** (9/2 op 4/1) 3 Parson's
Cross (6-11-3), 8 OCEANUS (btn 14l+) (9-10-10,
D Shaw), **improved into midfield halfway,
blundered and weakened six out.** (33/1 op 20/1);
14 Ran. 1½l, 4l, 2½l, 4l, 2l, hd. 6m 38.10s (a 25.10s).
RACECHECK: Wins 0, pl 1, unpl 7.
  Jan 10, Kelso, 3m nov chase, good to soft, £2,137:
1 Fish Quay (7-10-10), 2 Ambergate (9-10-10),
3 Traprain Law (7-11-3), U TARTAN TEMPEST
(7-11-3, G McCourt), **lost place and behind sixth,
blundered and unseated rider eighth.** (3/1 jt-fav op
5/2); 11 Ran. 1½l, 10l, 15l, 12l, 1½l. 6m 29.30s
(a 29.80s).
  Jan 2, Ayr, 3m 110y nov chase, good to soft,
£2,717: 1 Traprain Law (7-11-5), 2 Radical Lady (6-
11-0),3 Interim Lib (7-11-5), 4 TARTAN TEMPEST
(7-11-13, G McCourt), **prominent till outpaced
from four out, stayed on from two out.** (11/8 fav op
5/4 tchd 13/8); 9 Ran. 2½l, 10l, 1½l, hd, 12l. 6m
30.00s (a 26.50s).

ROMANY KING   6-11-4
34411-6B21212   **G B Balding**
br g Crash Course - Winsome Lady by Tarqogan
1988-89 2m 1f h good/soft (Devon); 2m 1f h
soft (Devon)
  1989-90 (Feb) 2¼m 110y ch soft (Fontwell)
nov; **(Mar)** 2l/2m ch good/soft (Chepstow)
nov Hcp [Open, 107,**97**]. £9,041 (£6,517).
LWR (89+90): **97** (2l)   TR: **101**
  March 22, Devon & Exeter, 2m 1f nov chase
[Open, 101], good to firm, £4,107: 1 Highfire
(8-11-2), 2 ROMANY KING (6-11-10, **101**, R Guest),
**held up, tracked leaders from five out, close
fourth when blundered next, ridden two out, not
quicken.** (6/5 fav op Events tchd 4/5) 3 Minim
(7-10-5); 8 Ran. 10l, nk, 12l, 12l, 4m 25.20s
(a 12.20s).
RACECHECK: Wins 2, pl 1, unpl 2.
  March 10, Chepstow, 2½m nov Hcp chase
[Open, 107], good to soft, £4,207: 1 ROMANY
KING (6-11-0, **97**, R Guest), **held up, mistake
12th, led three out, ran on well.** (7/2 tchd 9/2)
2 ASTRE RADIEUX (5-10-10, **93**, S Cowley),
**prominent, led four out to next, every chance
last, ran on.** (6/1 op 4/1) 3 Elvercone (9-10-12, v),
6 VALASSY (btn 27l) (7-10-13, **99**, N Williamson,3*),
**prominent till hard ridden and weakened four
out.** (14/1). F KILKILMARTIN (8-10-11, **94**,
M Richards), **started slowly, well behind to
halfway, good headway 11th, fourth and running
on when fell three out.** (5/1 op 4/1); 13 Ran.
2l, 7l, 5l, 12l, ¾l, 2l. 5m 7.50s (a 17.50s).
SR: 31/25/20/19/15/6.
RACECHECK: Wins 5, pl 3, unpl 4.
  March 1, Ludlow, 2½m nov chase, good to soft,
£2,869: 1 Shady Road (8-11-5), 2 ROMANY KING
(6-11-10, R Guest), **soon behind, ran on strongly
from two out, too much to do.** (5/2 fav op 9/4 tchd
3/1) 3 Elite Boy (8-11-12,3*); 16 Ran. 2l, hd, 15l, 8l,
8l. 5m 7.80s (a9.80s). SR: 23/26/30/-/-/-.
RACECHECK: Wins 2, pl 4, unpl 17.
  Feb 19, Fontwell, 2¼m 110 y nov chase, soft,
£2,310: 1 ROMANY KING (6-11-4, R Guest),
**always in touch, challenged from three out, led
last, held on well.** (9/4 fav op 5/2 tchd 3/1)
2 Master Comedy (6-10-11,7*), 3 KILKILMARTIN
(8-11-4, M Richards), **behind, headway and hit
11th, ran on from three out, kept on.** (33/1 op
20/1); 15 Ran. ¾l, 5l, 3l, ¾l, 2l, 10l, 3l, 8l. 4m 52.30s
(a 25.30s).

Figure 18(a)

THE HUMBLE TILLER   7-10-13
60/1F3222-41   N J Henderson

b g Rarity - Bardicate by Bargello **1988-89 2½m h good/soft (Southwell)**
1989-90 (Mar) 2m 5f ch good (Windsor) nov. **£4,174 (£2,836).**
LWR (89+90): -   TR: **96**

March 5, Windsor, 2m 5f nov chase, good, £2,836: 1 THE HUMBLE TILLER (7-11-2, R Dunwoody), **chased leaders, led approaching four out, stayed on under pressure run-in**. (9/4 fav op 2/1 tchd 11/4) 2 Bizage Motors (6-11-2), 3 Granny Pray On (8-10-6,5*); 18 Ran. 2l, 1l, 12l, 4l, 1½l, hd, 10l, 4l. 5m 22.00s (a 5.00s). SR: 7/5/-/-/-/-.
RACECHECK: Wins 2, pl 1, unpl 16.

Dec 21, Towcester, 2m 5f 110y nov chase, good, £2,210: 1 Castle Oaks (6-11-0), 2 Rambling Echo (8-11-0), 3 Another Striplight (6-10-7,7*), 4 THE HUMBLE TILLER (6-11-0, R Dunwoody), **pressed leaders till weakened after three out**. (7/2 fav op 7/4); 11 Ran. 7l, 8l, 7l, 8l. 5m 48.80s (a 18.80s).

April 27 1989, Towcester, 2m 5f 26y nov hdle, heavy, £1,088: 1 Market Forces (6-11-11), 2 THE HUMBLE TILLER (6-11-0, J Railton, 4*), **progress fifth, every chance two out, not quicken approaching last**. (11/8 fav op 5/4 tchd 6/4), 3 Idiot's Beauty (8-10-13); 17 Ran. 7l, 20l, 25l, 3l, dist. 5m 59.40s (a 52.40s).

FAMOUS LAD   7-11-5
6003/453-B12   R Lee

b g Bold Lad - Famous Band by Banderilla
1989-90 (Feb) 2m ch good/soft (Catterick) nov. **£2,228.**
LWR (89+90): -   TR: **102**

March 3, Hereford, 2m nov chase, soft, £2,721: 1 New Halen (9-11-7,7*), 2 FAMOUS LAD (7-11-6, R Bellamy,5*), **always going well, smooth headway to lead two out, blundered and pecked last, not recover**. (2/1 fav op 5/2) 3 Roman Dart (6-11-11); 13 Ran. 2½l, 12l, dist. 4m 9.90s (a 14.90s). SR: 23/17/5/-/-/-.
RACECHECK: Wins 1, pl 3, unpl 12.

Feb 21, Catterick, 2m nov chase, good to soft, £2,228: 1 FAMOUS LAD (7-11-2, D Dowling), **settled midfield, improved from three out to lead between last two, ran on well**. (20/1 op 16/1), 2 Mr Therm (5-10-4,3*), 3 Beau Guest (8-11-2,7*); 11 Ran. 3l, sh-hd, 5l, ½l, 4l. 4m 3.50s (a 12.50s).

Jan 23, Chepstow, 2½m nov chase, heavy, £3,195: 1 Elvercone (9-11-3,v), 2 Celtic Walk (6-11-9), 3 Regal Castle (7-11-3,bl), B FAMOUS LAD (7-11-3, B Dowling), **brought down first**. (33/1 op 25/1); 15 Ran. 12l, 1½l, 10l, 20l, ½l. 5m 32.00s (a 42.00s). SR: 9/3/-/-/-/-.

HOTPLATE   7-11-10
4330121052/142-1F5131P   D McCain

ch g Buckskin (FR) - Pencil Lady by Bargello **1987-88 2½m h soft (Newcastle); 2m 1f 110y h heavy (Carlisle) 1988-89 2½m h good/soft (Carlisle)**
1989-90 (Nov) 2m ch good (Haydock) nov; **(Feb) 2m ch good (Carlisle)** Hcp [0-125, 120,96]; **(Mar) 2m ch soft (Carlisle)** Hcp [Open, 130, 103]. **£14,587 (£10,004).**
LWR (89+90): **103** (5l)   TR: **107**

April 5, Liverpool, 3m 1f nov chase, good to firm, £21,036; 1 Royal Athlete (7-11-9), 2 Arctic Call (7-11-3,bl), 3 Cahervillahow (6-11-6), P HOTPLATE (7-11-3, M Dwyer), **soon outpaced, behind when pulled up before three out**. (50/1 op 33/1); 11 Ran. ½l, 10l, 15l, nk, 15l. 6m 11.30s (eq ave).
RACECHECK: Wins 0, pl 2, unpl 0.

March 9, Carlisle, 2m Hcp chase [Open,130], soft, £2,684: 1 HOTPLATE (7-10-4, inc 4lb ow, **103**, M Dwyer), **always going well, led after three out, ran on strongly**. (10/11 op 11/10) 2 Reiver's Lad (9-10-1), 3 Masnoon (7-12-30; 5 Ran. 5l, 3l, 2l, 20l. 4m 21.90s (a 20.90s).
RACECHECK: Wins 0, pl 1, unpl 7.

Feb 20, Sedgefield, 2½m Hcp chase [0-125,118], good to soft, £2,476: 1 Sword Beach (6-10-2), 2 Captain Mor (8-10-6), 3 HOTPLATE (7-10-5, 99, P Niven), **always well placed, every chance and ridden from last, one pace**. (3/1 tchd 7/2); 7 Ran. Nk, 4l, 25l, 15l, 15l. 5m 28.20s (a 20.20s). SR: 22/25/20/11/-/-.

LOUGH ROAD   8-10-12
252S/000205-P20F2   Mrs G E Jones

ch g Laurence O - Vixen's Red by Bargello
LWR (89+90): -   TR: **95**

April 4, Huntingdon, 3m chase, good to firm, £2,247: 1 Erostin Floats (6-11-7), 2 LOUGH ROAD (8-11-0, J Bryan), **chased leaders, led briefly three out, kept on one pace from next**. (7/2 op 4/1 tchd 9/2) 3 Short List (7-11-0); 9 Ran. 2l, 7l, 1½l, 30l. 6m 19.20s (a 30.20s).
RACECHECK: Wins 1, pl 1, unpl 3.

March 21, Worcester, 3m nov chase, good, £4,050: 1 Rambling Echo (9-11-10), 2 Croix de Guerre (9-11-10,bl), 3 Coruscate (8-11-10), F LOUGH ROAD (8-11-10, J Bryan), **always prominent, ridden 14th, challenging in third place when fell two out**. (7/1 op 6/1); 15 Ran. Nk, 12l, 10l, 15l, dist. 5m 59.40s (a 13.40s). SR: 22/21/9/-/-/-.
RACECHECK: Wins 0, pl 5, unpl 9.

Figure 18(b)

Analysis of this produced the following numbers shown in Figure 19 for later computation:

	A Prize money rating	B Form figure rating	C Position last time out	D 'Racecheck' places	E 'Racecheck' runs
Astre Radieux	25 (£25~~16~~)	6 (62÷10=6)	1 (1st)	11 (2+4+2+3)	25 (2+4+11+2+3+3)
Famous Lad	22	6	2	4	16
Hotplate	24	5	7	1	8
Lough Road	—	3	2	2	5
Romany King	23	6	2	17	40
The Humble Tiller	21	7	1	3	19
Tartan Tempest	15	4	2	1	8

Figure 19

The five numbers given above for each of the seven runners, when subjected to the key-pressing procedure (already described earlier in relation to Only Trouble) produced the following ratings:

> Astre Radieux   36.33   won 8/1
> Romany King   33.87   2nd 8/1
> Famous Lad   25.49
> The Humble Tiller   20.64
> Hotplate   16.58
> Tartan Tempest   14.57
> Lough Road   6.32

The full result, as given in the *Daily Mail* was:

> **2.00** (2m 5f Hcap Ch) – **ASTRE RADIEUX** (M Perrett) **8-1, 1; Romany King** (R Guest) **8-1, 2; Bantel Buccaneer** (T Reed) **25-1, 3. Tartan Tempest** (N Doughty) **8-1, 4. 18 ran.** 11-2 JtFav The Humble Tiller, (S Mellor, Swindon) 8, 5. **Tote:** £6.20: £1.50, £1.90, £5.80, £2.00. DF: £7.30. CSF: £66.23. Tricast: £1,415.93. NR: Western Legend, Moiety.

Figure 20

Readers may want to use their pocket calculator to make selections by working on ratings that appear, not in specialised racing newspapers, but in daily ones such as the *Mirror*, the *Daily Mail*, the *Sun*, the *Daily Star*, the *Daily Express*, *The Times* and the *Guardian*.

Some of these publications fail to give some of the information necessary to amend their own performance ratings, so as to take account of race fitness and suitability of course, distance and going in the manner already recommended. Neither do they make such amendments in an undisclosed manner.

However, the backer should amend whatever ratings are featured by applying the same sequence of key-pressing routines that have just been described to what every daily or evening paper always includes in its particular coverage of racing – the form lines of individual contestants.

This sequence, which forms the cornerstone of all the selection methods featured in this book, is shown in Figure 21.

1. Enter the newspaper performance rating for a runner.

2. Press + key.

3. Enter a betting forecast figure (10 for a favourite, 9 for a second favourite, and so on).

4. Press – key.

5. Enter figure showing horse's finishing position last time out – i.e. 1 for a win, 2 for a second, etc. NB A 'duck's egg' (0) should be entered as 7.

6. Press = key.

7. Press × key.

8. From the horse's complete form line, enter the total number of times that the horse won or was placed second or third in all races shown. If any of these races were run in a previous season they should be included in the calculations.

9. Press = key.

10. Press × key.

11. Enter 100.

12. Press ÷ key.

13. Enter total number of digits shown in horse's form line.

14. Press = key.

15. Press √ key.

16. Note down horse's final rating.

Figure 21

EXAMPLE ONE: the *Daily Express*:

This newspaper is particularly useful to the serious follower of horse racing since it is the only non-specialist daily that features the selections of both the private handicapper responsible for the 'W' factor form ratings and and an assessor of race times. It also includes the choices of a computer programmer called 'Computerman'.

The work of the expert who compiles the 'W' factor rating is given the most comprehensive coverage in the *Daily Express* and the figures he provides are those best suited to pocket-calculator computations that involve the, perhaps by now rather familiar 16-step button-pressing process that produced the earlier rating of Only Trouble and the selection of 8–1 winner, Astre Radieux.

5.00–HEATHROW MAIDEN STAKES
£4,232 (D)   1m   (8)

601 (3)	5-55092	● INVADER (14) C Brittain *(2)*4 9 7	.P Robinson	★78
602 (8)	4	TACHOMETER (14) H Howe *(32)*6 9 2	.A Nicholls(3)	59
603 (5)		CONWY CASTLE J Gosden *(6)*3 8 13	.R Havlin	–
604 (7)	75-0478	FREDDY FLINTSTONE (15) R Hannon *(2)*3 8 13	.D O'Neill	72
605 (6)	58-6464	HAMLYN (5) D Elsworth *(5)*3 8 13	.K Darley	76
606 (4)	4	ALTARA (19) W Muir *(6)*3 8 8	.M Dwyer	64
607 (2)		DANZIG WITHWOLVES (F) H Cecil *(3)*3 8 8	.T Quinn	–
608 (1)		WOOLFE (F) J Gosden *(6)*3 8 8	.J Fortune	–

BLINKERS: No. 5 VISOR: No. 1.

Express Betting Forecast: — 9-4 Danzig Withwolves, 7-2 Invader, 4 Freddy Flintstone, 5 Woolfe, 7 Hamlyn, 10 Conwy Castle, 16 Tachometer, 20 Altara.

1999: Silver Apple (6) 3-8-13 K Darley 7-1 (P Cole) 10 ran.

GUIDE: There are encouraging reports from Newmarket concerning **DANZIG WITH-WOLVES**, a $900,000 yearling, whose dam was a classy performer in America. Jockey bookings suggest **Woolfe**, related to several useful types, is the yard's first string. Of those with experience Invader should be winning before long, judged on his head second to Argentan (run well since) at Doncaster. There is better to come from **Altara**, fourth to Daniysha at Chepstow (7f) but may need even further. The return to this trip should suit **Freddy Flintstone**, whose fourth to Atavus in a mile Newmarket handicap is solid. **Hamlyn** has the ability but is not a straightforward ride. *DRAW BIAS: None.*   JR

5.00–Invader (P Robinson, 11-2) 1; Freddy Flintstone (5-1, 2nd fav) 2; Woolfe (10-1) 3. 8 ran. Nk, 1¼l. (C Brittain; Danzig Withwolves 8-11 fav). **Tote:** £6.60; pl £1.40, £1.30, £1.90; ex £26; trifecta £92.10; csf £30.28.

Figure 22

For example, on Thursday 27 July 2000, this process, as usual, involved points being given to each runner for, respectively, its newspaper form rating, position in the betting forecast, last time out placing and the proportion of instances in its form line when it had been placed in the first three. The pocket calculator's processing of these points pinpointed an 11–2 winner in the final race at Sandown Park which was preferred to any other at this principal meeting because it involved an ideal number of eight runners and, unlike races run over other distances on this course, did not involve any draw bias.

As readers may care to check, the 16-step button-pressing process left Invader with a top rating of 37.63. Incidentally, confidence in Invader was increased by the fact that he was also the 'spot' selection of the time expert of the *Daily Express*, as can be seen in Figure 22.

EXAMPLE TWO: the *Sun*

The large circulation of this newspaper means that it is consulted by many a fan of horse racing. Thus it is fortunate that within its pages the 'Sport of Kings' is given comprehensive and uncontroversial treatment. As for this particular paper's form services, 'Sunform' is a concise and fairly extensive form summary which usefully incorporates race-readers' comments.

Even more usefully for those interested in computational approaches to finding winners, a further form service known as 'Sunratings' accords a score of 99 (as in its Murdoch-owned stable-mate *The Times*) to a runner top-rated according to this particular private handicap. These ratings have, on occasion, proved highly accurate.

Indeed, in one recent six-month period Sunratings top-rated 1057 horses, of which 407, or 38 per cent , were actually successful!

One recent 'Sunratings' selection, made on 2 August 2000, after following the 'usual' 16-step computational process, involved Aegean Dream at Goodwood. The horse's final rating of 87.42 left him well clear of his rivals, which was this four-year-old's fate on the racecourse, where he won at 5–1.

4.25 WEATHERBYS BANK FILLIES' STAKES
to the winner £11,180; 1m 1f.   (10 runners)

501	(8)	9241814	**FREDORA 11 (D)** M Blanshard 5-10-0 . . . . .D Sweeney	92
502	(7)	2344331	**AEGEAN DREAM 11 (D)** R Hannon 4-9-9 . . . . .R Hughes ●99	
503	(9)	521	**TANGO TWO THOUSAND 23** J Gosden 3-9-5 . . . . .R Havlin	86
504	(6)	82-9011	**FAIR IMPRESSION 17** E Dunlop 3-9-4 . . . . .J Reid	92
505	(1)	532-317	**MUSCHANA 25** J Dunlop 3-9-1 . . . . .T Quinn	93
506	(4)	0-21061	**ROSHANI 12** M Channon 3-8-13 . . . . .Craig Williams	85
507	(10)	1270-00	**PHOEBE BUFFAY 11** C Allen 3--8-6 . . . . .Dane O'Neill	84
508	(5)	9912005	**DEN'S JOY 4 (D)** Miss D McHale 4-8-5 . . . . .K Darley	95
509	(3)	-042111	**PERFECT MOMENT 42 (D)** C Dwyer 3-7-13 . . . . .J Mackay (5)	86
510	(2)	3-76104	**COMMON CONSENT 9** S Woodman 4-7-11 . . . . .F Norton	95

SUN BETTING: 7-2 Tango Two Thousand, 4 Aegean Dream, 5 Fair Impression, 6 Fredora, 8 Muschana, Perfect Moment, 10 Roshani, Den's Joy.

> **4.25** (1m 1f Hcap) – **AEGEAN DREAM**
> (R Hughes) **5-1 (2ndFav)** 1; **Common
> Consent 14-1** 2; **Muschana 13-2** 3.
> **10 ran.** 4-1 Fav Tango Two Thousand.
> (R Hannon). 2, shd. **Tote:** £6.10; £21.00,
> £3.60, £2.70. Ex: £72.50. CSF: £63.80.
> Trifecta: £1,225.30. Tricast: £425.06.

Figure 23

EXAMPLE THREE: the *Guardian*

It is only fairly recently that this newspaper has included ratings in its form coverage but these, on occasion, can prove highly accurate, especially when refined by means of the pocket calculator. For example, on Monday 31 July 2000, amendment by calculator of the following *Guardian* ratings for a Yarmouth race meant that a Computer Straight Forecast (CSF) of £23.54 was landed when top-rated Presentofarose (with 68.55 points) defeated Banningham Blitz (second rated with 57.15 points).

6.55	E.D.P. Best For Jobs Selling Stakes 2YO		
	6f 3yds/£1,845		
1 (4) 0	**Hard To Cash (6)** D Cosgrove 8.11	**L Newton**	—
2 (3) 654302	**Banningham Bliz (6)** D Shaw 8.6	**J Quinn**	★90
3 (2)	**Mrs Mitchell** D Nicholls 8.6	**G Bardwell**	—
4 (6) 502343	**Presentofarose (7)** J S Moore 8.6	**J Mackay (5)**	89
5 (5)	**Teenawon** K Burke 8.6	**N Callan**	—
6 (1) 4466	**Unveil (11)** G McCourt 8.6	**D O'Donohoe**	85

Betting   6–4 Banningham Bliz, 7–4 Unveil, 6–1 Presentofarose, 8–1Mrs Mitchell, 14–1 Teenawon, 20–1 Hard to Cash.

Figure 24(a)

6.55　E.D.P. Best for Jobs Selling
[OFF 6.55]　Stakes (Class G)　　　　(6f3y) 6f

For: 2-y-o **1st** £1,844.50 2nd £527 3rd £263.50

1　　**PRESENTOFAROSE (IRE)** (6) 2 8-1　...(43) **J Mackay**(5)
　　　　b f by Presenting–Little Red Rose (Precocious)
　　　　(J S Moore) *made virtually all, headed briefly inside final furlong,*
　　　　outbattled errant rival close home [op 8/1 tchd 9/1 in places] **7/1**

2　　½ **BANNINGHAM BLIZ** (3) 2 8-6 b ....(50)　　　J Quinn
　　　　ch f by Inchinor–Mary From Dunlow (Nicholas Bill)
　　　　(D Shaw) *behind, ridden halfway, closed gradually to lead briefly*
　　　　inside final furlong, shirked issue and threw it away　　[bet of
　　　　£2,200-£800]　　　　　　　　　　　　　[tched 5/2] **11/4**

3　　*3* TEENAWON (IRE) (5) 2 8-6 .... N Callan
　　　　ch f by Polar Falcon (USA)–Oasis (Valiyar)
　　　　(K R Burke) *started slowly and ran green, headway over 1f out,*
　　　　no impression inside　　　　[op 3/1 tchd 9/2 in places] **4/1**

4　　1¾ HARD TO CASH (IRE) (4) 2 8-11 .... L Newton
　　　　(D J S Cosgrove) *close up, ridden halfway, ran on one pace final*
　　　　furlong　　　　　　　　[op 16/1 tchd 20/1] **14/1**

5　　*10* UNVEIL (1) 2 8-6 .... (57)D O'Donohoe
　　　　(G M McCourt) *prominent, driven halfway, no response and*
　　　　beaten well over 1f out [bet of £1,000-£400(x2)]　[op 9/4] **5/2F**

6　　1¾ MRS MITCHELL (2) 2 8-6 .... G Bardwell
　　　　(D Nicholls) *dwelt, soon chasing leaders, driven and faded over*
　　　　2f out　　　　　　　　　　　　　　**5/1**

6 ran　　**TIME** 1m 16.70s (slow by 4.30s)　**SP TOTAL PERCENT** 111

1st OWNER: Chris Bradbury BRED: S Twomey

TRAINER: J S Moore at East Garston, Berks

2nd OWNER: Crown Select

3rd OWNER: Haydn D Kelly

TOTE WIN £5.00; PL £2.10, £2.00; EX £17.70; CSF £23.54

The winner was bought for 3,250 guineas

Figure 24(b)

EXAMPLE FOUR: the *Daily Mail*

In his widely read guide to horse-race selection and betting, author Peter Braddock recommends the *Daily Mail* for the excellence of its racing coverage, of which an impressive part is represented by 'Formcast' – a set of private-handicap ratings.

BIG-RACE FIELD

3.20—CHAMPAGNE LANSON SUSSEX STAKES (GROUP 1) (CLASS A) £250,000 added (£159,500) 1m (10)   **BBC2**

301 (10) 1/214-14 **ALJABR 43** Saeed bin Suroor 4-9-7 . . . . .R Hills **73**
Runs: 8 Wins: 5 (C&DCDBF) (GS) Places: 1
4l 4th to Kalanisi in the Queen Anne Stakes (1m) under a Group One penalty

302 (1) 4320-36 **ALMUSHTARAK 74** K Mahdi 7-9-7 . . . . .T Quinn **68**
Runs: 41 Wins 5 (D3) (GS) Places: 16
5¾l 6th to Ajabr in the Group One Lockinge Stakes (1m) at Newbury

303 (8) 38-4841 **ARKADIAN HERO 32** L Cumani 5-9-7 . . . . .J P Spencer **71**
Runs: 21 Wins: 6 (C) (G) Places: 2
Beat Chagali by 2l in Group Three race at Newmarket (7f)

304 (3) 133-112 **DANSILI 43** A Fabre(Fr) 4-9-7 . . . . .O Peslier●**78**
Runs: 10 Wins: 5 (D5) (S) Places: 4
½l 2nd to Kalanisi (receiving 3lb) in the Queen Anne Stakes

305 (4) 31/123-1 **JOSR ALGARHOUD 38** Saeed bin Suroor 4-9-7 .J Reid **65**
Runs: 6 Wins: 3 (G) Places: 3
Won Group Three race at Longchamp (7f) on belated reappearance

306 (9) 2-04185 **GOLDEN SILCA 21** M Channon 4-9-4 . . .Craig Williams **67**
Runs: 18 Wins: 6 (DBF) (GS) Places: 5
Well beaten 8th in the Queen Anne and worse off at these weights

307 (6) 1-1221 **GIANT'S CAUSEWAY 25** A P O'Brien (Ire) 3-9-0
Runs: 8 Wins: 6 (D) (GS) Places: 2   **M J Kinane 77**
Game head winner from Kalanisi in Group One Eclipse (10f) at Sandown

308 (7) 1-1 **MANHATTAN 62** A P O'Brien (Ire) 3-9-0 . . .Paul Scallan **40**
Runs: 2 Wins: 2 (S) Places: 0
Made all to narrowly win a small race at Tipperary (9f)

309 (2) 31130 **MEDICEAN 18** Sir M Stoute 3-9-0 . . . . .J Murtagh **64**
Runs: 5 Wins: 2 (D2BF) (GS) Places: 2
No impression when favourite for the John Smith's Cup Handicap (10f)

310 (5) 14-32 **VALENTINO 43 (T)** J Gosden 3-9-0 . . . . .G Mosse **65**
Runs: 4 Wins: 1 (G) Places: 2
Head 2nd to Giant's Causeway in Group One St James's Palace Stakes (1m)

Probable SP: 11–4 Giant's Causeway, 3 Dansili, 7–2 Ajabr, 5 Valentino, 8 Arkadian Hero, 10 Medicean, 16 Josr Algarhoud, 33 Almushtarak, Manhattan.

FAVOURITES: 3 3 1 0 2 3 2 0 2 1   **AGES: 4 3 3 3 3 5 4 4 4 3**

3.20—Giant's Causeway (M J Kinane, 3–1 jt-fav) 1; Dansili (3–1 jt-fav) 2; Medicean (12–1) 3. 10 ran. ¾l, 1½l, (A P B'Brien). **Tote:** £3.50; pl £1.50, £1.60, £2.60; ex £10.70; trifecta £89.80; csf £10.03.

Figure 25

As it happens, I have kept a now-yellowing copy of an article on 'Formcast' in which it is claimed that its ratings are likely to work out best in races carrying the most prize money. Thus, on every racing day, I always rate the most valuable race at the main meeting – a procedure true to the very first principle of racehorse selection that was discussed in an earlier chapter on race selection.

For example , on Wednesday 2 August 2000, the Sussex Stakes at Goodwood was the day's principal race. After amending the 'Formcast' ratings for this event, Giant's Causeway emerged as top-rated with 92.73 from Dansili with 92.19 and these two high-class horses finished just as the amended ratings suggested they would, to land yet another CSF of £10.03.

EXAMPLE FIVE: the *Daily Star*

Since the *Daily Star* bills itself as the newspaper that's 'light years ahead', it is not surprising that it offers readers of its racing page something rather distinctive, if not exactly 'out of sight'! Indeed, the ratings appended to the names of many of the day's runners are as unusual as those in *The Times* in that they are based on time, rather than past form. This, in fact, explains why these ratings sometimes differ greatly from those of form experts of other newspapers amongst whom there is often a broad consensus as to runners 'best in' at the weights.

The 'Clockform' ratings in the *Daily Star* are, in fact, supplied by Split Second, the time expert of Raceform's weekly update. But, for the particular benefit of *Daily Star* readers, horses that have not previously run fast enough to be accorded a lowly speed figure of 40 are given a rating based on 'recent form and other factors'.

Any agreement betweeen Clockform and Starform – the non-ratings form service that the *Daily Star* also offers – should indicate horses whose form may well be worth subjecting to further computation. Such agreement was detectable on Friday 4 August 2000 at Goodwood and so the Clockform ratings for the race involved formed the starting point for the usual 16-step key-pressing sequence. This resulted in Flak Jacket in the 5.35 with 63.13 points emerging as top-rated and this sprinter duly won his race at 7–4.

5.35 STEWARDS' SPRINT STAKES
Class B   6f   (16 runners) £17,290

1	(3)	5-05102	**COMPTON BANKER (5)(G)** G A Butler 3 9 8 ....**P Doe**	79
2	(6)	00-0002	**SHAROURA (2)(D,F,S)** D Nicholls 4 9 7 ....**R Hughes**	61
3	(4)	1125222	**TEYAAR (44)(D3,A)** D Shaw 4 9 6 ....**I Mongan(5)**	57
4	(12)	0310520	**SMART PREDATOR (20)(F,S)** J J Quinn 4 9 6 ....**M Tebbutt**	64
5	(2)	0000331	**ZUHAIR (2)(CD, C2, D3, A, F)** D Nicholls 7 9 6(5ex) ....**Alex Greaves**	51
6	(1)	1000306	**FRANCPORT (23)(D,S)** A Berry 4 9 5 ....**T Quinn**	56
7	(5)	0001130	**BOANERGES (7)(CD,F)** R Guest 3 9 5 ....**K Darley**	67
8	(15)	3313166	**CORUNNA (15)(D,F)** A Berry 3 9 5 ....**G Carter**	62
9	(10)	0000500	**PETRUS (5)(C,F,G)(T)** C Brittain 4 9 4 ....**Pat Eddery**	52
10	(8)	0563210	**DOUBLE OSCAR (14)(C,D3,A,F,G,S)(B)** D Nicholls 7 9 3	
			A Nicholls(3)	60
11	(11)	0210040	**GDANSK (14)(S)** A Berry 3 9 1 ....**J Carroll**	61
12	(7)	0052660	**REFERENDUM (2)(CD,S)** D Nicholls 6 9 1 ....**F Norton**	74
13	(9)	0-61060	**DIAMOND DECORUM (9)(D2,F,S)** P Evans 4 9 0 ....**M Roberts**	56
14	(14)	14000-1	**MISS HIT (113)(D,A,F,G,S)** G A Butler 5 8 13 ....**J P Spencer**	60
15	(16)	0000211	**FLAK JACKET (9)(D3,F,S)(T)** D Nicholls 5 8 6 ....**D Holland** ★85	
16	(13)	-005000	**STATOYORK (2)(F,S)** D Shaw 7 8 2 ....**D McCabe**	75

LONG HANDICAP: Zuhair 9-1.

Star Betting: — 4 Compton Banker, 5 Flak Jacket, 11-2 Zuhair, 10 Sharoura, Double Oscar, Miss Hit, 12 Francport, 14 others.

1999: ZUHAIR, 6-9-11(5ex), (Alex Greaves, 9-1) D Nicholls, drawn (8), 18 ran.

STARFORM: FLAK JACKET Danger: Zuhair

5.35 (6f Hcap) — **FLAK JACKET** (D Holland) **7–4 Fav** 1; **Referendum 25–1** 2; **Smart Predator 20–1** 3; **Compton Banker 9–2 (2ndFav)** 4. **16 ran.** (D Nicholls). 1, ½, 2. **Tote:** £2.80; £1.30, £5.80, £4.30, £1.80. Ex: £108.40. CSF: £57.99. Trifecta: £2,678.20. Tricast: £678.28.

Figure 26

EXAMPLE SIX: the *Mirror*

This newspaper's form coverage includes ' Spotform' ratings which do not appear in raw form but are already adjusted to take account of such crucial race-day factors as the draw, the going, the distance, the course in question, jockeyship, the trainer's past record, as well as the wearing of blinkers and other aids to concentration.

With these factors taken into account, as well as a runner's recent form and its temperament, the private handicap weights that originally formed the starting point for Spotform become ratings that have become so finely tuned and adjusted that one horse always emerges as a clear top-rated selection.

The basic belief of the Spotform team is that whatever a horse has already achieved, it may well, given similar circumstances, accomplish again and the singularly refined nature of the final figures they provide means that further adjustments to these should result in some sophisticated final scores.

A Spotform rating appears on the extreme right of the full form entry for each runner, as can be seen in Figure 27.

If the 16-step key-pressing routine, already described, is applied to the above ratings, it will be found that, with 64.54 points in the above Goodwood race, Murghem was predicted to prevail. This contender duly trotted up at 5–2.

4.25 –GLORIOUS TIOMAN ISLAND RATED STAKES
(A) 1m 4f Winner £29,000 (7 run)

1   242111   **MURGHEM (34)** 1 M Johnston 5 9 7 **(Gd, D, SF)** ....**D Holland 41**
            Made all, stayed on Newm't 1½m (A), beat Double Eclipse a nk
2   10/1211- **VICIOUS CIRCLE (313)** 7 L Cumani 6 9 6 **(Gd, Hy, D)** ......**J P Spencer —**
            Ran on Ascot 1½m (B) Sept, beat Ligne Gagnante (rec 22lb) 3½l
3   39-0241   **LIGHTNING ARROW (USA) (14)** 6 J Dunlop 4 9 5 **(Gd, D, F)** ....**T Quinn 39**
            Led 3f out at Newmarket 1½m (C), beating Rain In Spain 4l
4   32-6022   **LIGNE GAGNANTE (21)** 5 W Haggas 4 8 7 **(Gd, CD, BF)** .....**K Darley 42 ●**
            Hampered 2f out when 3l 2nd of 9 to Boreas at York 1½m (B)
5   434824-   **BALLADONIA (295)** 4 Lady Herries 4 8 7 **(Gd, C)** ....**J Reid —**
            Chance 2f out, 4½l 4th of 14 to Katiykha 1½m Newmarket (B)
6   7412-50   **FAIR WARNING (GER) (80)** 2 J Hills 4 8 7 **(Gd, D)** ....**M Hills 39**
            Behind final 3f, distant last of 17 to Inch Perfect at York 1½m (C)
7   414930   **JUST IN TIME (28)** 3 T Mills 5 8 7 **(Gd, C)** ....**L Carter 40**
            Held 2f out, 15l 14th to Lady Angharad at Sandown 1¼m (B)

Betting: 9–4 Murghem, 11–4 Vicious Circle, 7–2 Lightning Arrow, 9–2 Ligne Gagnante,
9 Balladonia, 16 Just In Time, 25 Fair Warning

Figure 27

4.25 (1m 4f Hcap) — **MURGHEM** (D Holland) **5-2 Fav** 1; **Lightning Arrow 9-2** 2; **Ligne Gagnante 7-2 (2ndFav)** 3. **7 ran.** (M Johnston). ½, 1¼. **Tote:** £3.30; £2.30, £2.50. Ex: £15.60. CSF: £11.58

Figure 28

EXAMPLE SEVEN: *The Times*

Lastly, it would seem appropriate that, in a final bid to help to refine the ratings offered in the various racing pages of daily newspapers, I try to 'go out with a bang' by suggesting how those of the 'Thunderer' might be profitably exploited by adjusting the ratings they contain on a pocket calculator.

Computing the chances of runners in valuable races that *The Times'* private handicapper has rated is often profitable, as on 4 August 2000 at Goodwood in the 3.50. After the usual round of button-pressing, Misty Eyed, with 78.61 points, emerged as top-rated and duly won at 3–1.

3.50 THE QUEEN MOTHER'S 100TH BIRTHDAY MOLECOMB STAKES   BBC2
(Group III: 2-Y-O: £24,000: 5f) (10 runners)

1	(3)	41410	TARAS EMPEROR 45 (D,S) (Tara Leisure) J J Quinn 9-1 ....J Fortune	88
2	(5)	322122	BOUNCING BOWDLER 43 (D,G) (P Dean) M Johnston 8-12 ....D Holland	83
3	(10)	222	CHARLIE PARKES 71 (BF) (J Heler) A Berry 8-12 ....J Carroll	78
4	(9)	61	PICCLED 64 (CD,S) (Capt J Macdonald-Buchanan) M Channon 8-12 ....T Quinn	57
5	(8)	620	REEL BUDDY 13 (Speedlith Group) R Hannon 8-12 ....R Hughes	70
6	(7)	211100	SHOESHINE BOY 13 (D,S) (Oneoneone Racing) B Meehan 8-12.......Pat Eddery	85
7	(1)	36105	SPEEDY GEE 14 (D,F) (J Guest) M Channon 8-12 ....Craig Williams	76
8	(6)	51011	MISTY EYED 26 (D,F) (Mrs J Fuller) Mrs P Dutfield 8-10......................L Newman	95
9	(4)	511132	ELSIE PLUNKETT 13 (D,F,S) (C J M Partnership) R Hannon 8-7 ....Dane O'Neil	89
10	(2)	121211	RED MILLENNIUM 21 (D,F,G,S) (Red Shirt Brigade Ltd) A Berry 8-7.......F Norton	88

BETTING: 3–1 Bouncing Bowdler, 7–2 Misty Eyed, 5–1 Elsie Plunkett, 6–1 Charlie Parkes, Red Millennium, 10–1 Shoeshine Boy, Taras Emperor, 20–1 others.

1999: MISTY MISS 8–7 J F Egan (33–1) P Evans 10 ran

3.50 (5f 2yo) — MISTY EYED (L Newman) 3-1 Fav 1; Bouncing Bowdler 7-2 (2ndFav) 2; Red Millennium 5-1 3. 9 ran. (Mrs P Dutfield). 1¼, 1¾. Tote: £3.90; £1.60, £1.80, £1.40. Ex: £15.90. CSF: £12.00. Tf: £33.70. NR: Charlie Parkes

Figure 29

CHAPTER 3

CALCULATING WHEN TO BET FROM BETTING SHOWS

Having used a calculator to select the race on any racing day that is most suitable for investment purposes and actually to make a selection in it, the backer should again employ electronics to calculate exactly when to make a wager.

Interestingly, *When To Bet and Win* was the name given to a once best-selling work which advised backers how to do so. I can only endorse the view of its author that, if they know when to get involved, backers can exercise the same businesslike control of their activities that is the cornerstone of successful bookmaking.

As was recently pointed out in an advertisement for a 'revolutionary new concept in betting', in the business transacted between backers and bookmakers, the latter have a built-in advantage. This helps to explain why, in archetypal terms, bookmakers have long been seen, if rather erroneously, as cigar-smoking, rather flashily dressed and ostentatiously wealthy owners of large cars with personalised number plates. However, the racing enthusiast must be aware of the methods of the bookmaker and adopt evasive ploys.

If 'armed' with a pocket calculator in a betting shop, on a racecourse or in an armchair, one can rapidly check the prices that make up successive betting shows and so determine when a book – that is, a complete set of prices for a race – is no longer excessively, and thus unfairly, 'over-round'.

The calculations concerned here involve dividing the right-hand side of each runner's odds by the sum of both sides. Thus 7–4 becomes 4 ÷ 11. Separate calculations need to be made for every runner in the race and the resultant decimal fractions added together to give a final total. An example from an actual race is given in Figure 30 .

Odds	Calculation needed	Result
6–4	4 ÷ 10	0.4000
11–4	4 ÷ 15	0.2667
7–2	2 ÷ 9	0.2222
6–1	1 ÷ 7	0.1429
25–1	1 ÷ 26	0.0385
	Total	1.0703

Figure 30

The result, after moving the decimal point two places to the right, is 107.03. Thus, the bookmaker is working to 107 per cent, his book is 7 per cent 'over-round' and he is offering backers overall value for money. In fact, a book that is only 'over-round' by 15 per cent or less is a rather rare occurence and one that is most likely to arise when prices are being quoted against the runners in a small field. Often in races in which a large field faces the starter, the odds quoted against the chances of fancied contestants may be reasonably tempting, yet outsiders could well be on offer at very cramped rates. What frequently results is a book that is extremely and very unfairly 'over-round'.

If degrees of 'over-roundness' of under 15 per cent are discovered by this rapid calculation, one should waste no time in 'getting on' before, as is fairly likely, the trading position becomes far less favourable. Very often it will be found that bookmakers (who work to marked cards indicating by means of a cross, a dot and a capital C, the likely first and second favourites and a third runner about which they are warned to be 'careful') recognise their initial vulnerability and so start to trade at rates that are distinctly ungenerous. Frequently, the opening show will, in fact, feature prices that prove to be 'over-round' by well over 20 per cent.

If this is the case, one should patiently note the opening prices and hope for some general improvement in the trading position. This will often occur, as is illustrated in Figure 31 which shows exactly how the odds quoted against the runners in an actual eight-horse race fluctuated between the first show and the close of trading. It provides most convincing proof of the wisdom of using an electronic calculator in an attempt to play and, with luck, beat the bookmakers at their own 'numbers game'. The over-round numbers arrived at in Figure 31 result from the division process shown in Figure 30 followed by the moving of the decimal point two places to the right.

	Over-round Calculation Odds at First Show			Over-round Calculation Odds at Final Show	
A	4–7	63.64		4–5	55.56
B	7–2	22.22		9–2	18.18
C	5–1	16.67		7–1	12.50
D	5–1	16.67		9–1	10.00
E	16–1	5.88		12–1	7.67
F	16–1	5.88		25–1	3.85
G	16–1	5.88		25–1	3.85
H	20–1	4.76		33–1	2.94
		Total 141.60			Total 114.55
		Over-round 41.60			Over-round 14.55

Figure 31

Backers who are of the opinion that when money 'talks' in racing, it does so just as revealingly as it does in many other spheres of human activity, may wish to use their calculators to determine from betting shows, rather than from racing form, precisely which contender to support.

Firstly, it should be pointed out that if on the race-track, or on a television screen at home, or in a betting shop, backers notice that well-fancied, short-priced horses have their opening odds untrimmed or only marginally so, while an outsider has its opening rate cut by a considerable proportion, they may have spotted a potentially profitable development, as is illustrated in the following two race returns in which the one-eyed Monacle should have opened the eyes of backers to the fact that his were the only odds that shortened and, in the other race, Bad As I Wanna Be advanced in the betting from his opening odds of 10–1 to 6–1

– a reduction (calculated as representing 40 per cent) – that transpired by virtue, not of the imitative behaviour that so characterises the backers of favourites, but quite conceivably because of the fairly heavy weight of genuinely inspired support for this eventual attractively priced winner.

6.00 What's On Handicap
[OFF 6.00] **(Class E)** 2m

For: 3-y-o and up Rated 0–70 **1st** £3,493.75 2nd £1,075 3rd £537.50 4th £268.75

1   **MONACLE (1)** 6 8-10 . . . .**(36) R Mullen**
b g by Saddlers' Hall (IRE)–Endless Joy (Law Society (USA))
(John Berry) *dropped out last until straight, riden 3f out, steady run to lead 350 yards out, soon clear, ran on well*
[tchd 11/1 in places] **10/1**

2   3½ **XELLANCE (IRE) (6)** 3 9-4 . . . .**(66)** K Dalgleish(5)
b g by Be My Guest (USA)–Excellent Alibi (USA) (Exceller (USA))
(M Johnston) *settled 3rd, led 4f out, ridden 3f out, headed 350 yards out, one paced and soon beaten* [bets of even £1,500(x2), even £1,000(x3), even £600, £2,000-£2,200, £500-£550 (x2), £500-£600 and £400-£500(x3)]
[op 4/5 after evens in places] **Evens F**

3   5 BAISSE D'ARGENT (IRE) (7) 4 9-10 . . . . .**(50)** G Carter
b g by Common Grounds–Fabulous Pet (Somethingfabulous (USA))
(D J S Cosgrove) *never really on bridle, chased leaders, effort and ridden over 3f out, little response and ran on one pace*
[op 10/1] **14/1**

4   2½ NICIARA (IRE) (3) 3 7-8 b . . . .**(44)** Joanna Badger(7)
(M C Chapman) *led 12f, weakened over 2f out* [op 11/2] **6/1**

5   1 NUBILE (5) 6 8-8 tb . . . . **(34)** L Newton
(W J Musson) *behind, ridden over 4f out, plodded on and soon beaten* [op 12/1] **16/1**

6   10 RUM BABA (IRE) (4) 6 8-8 b . . . .**(39)** J Mackay(5)
(Mrs M Reveley) *pressed leader 12f, soon ridden, weakened over 2f out, eased and tailed off* [op 11/2 tchd 6/1] **9/2**

7   3½ RAYWARE BOY (IRE) (2) 4 8-13 b . . . .**(39)** N Callan
(D Shaw) *held up, in touch 4f, driven along and soon no response, tailed off* [op 25/1] **33/1**

7 ran   **TIME** 3m 33.20s (slow by 9.30s)   **SP TOTAL PERCENT** 107

1st OWNER: Chris Benest BRED: Cheveley Park Stud Ltd
TRAINER: John Berry at Newmarket, Suffolk
2nd OWNER: TT Bloodstocks
3rd OWNER: Winning Circle Racing Club
TOTE WIN £12.90; PL £3.70, £2.00; EX £37.60; CSF £16.37

Figure 32(a)

6.10   Fedora Maiden Stakes (Class D)

[OFF 6.11]   **(5f10y) 5f**

For: 2-y-o **1st £3,737.50** 2nd £1,150 3rd £575 4th £287.50

1   **BAD AS I WANNA BE (IRE)** (6) 2 9-0 . . . . .J **Fortune**
ch c Common Grounds–Song Of The Glens (Horage)
(B J Meehan) *made all, ridden out inside final 2f, readily* [bets of
£2,000-£320 each-way. £10,000-£1,800]
[op 6/1 after 10/1 and 8/1 in places, tchd 5/1] **6/1**

2   3 **SENIOR MINISTER** (16) 2 9-0 . . . . .J Tate
b c by Lion Cavern (USA)–Crime Ofthecentury (Pharly (FR))
(J M P Eustace) *started slowly, soon recovered to chase leaders,*
stayed on under pressure from over 1f out, went 2nd inside last,
no impression on winner [bet of £10,000-£1,200]   [tchd 8/1] **7/1**

3   1½ **HAWK** (1) 2 9-0 t . . . . .R Hughes
b c by A P Jet (USA)–Miss Enjoleur (USA) (L'Enjoleur (CAN))
(R Hannon) *pressed winner, ridden along from 2f out, one pace*
inside last [bets of £14,000-£4,000, £1,400-£400,
£3,000-£900(x2), £2,000-£600, £9,000-£3,000, £3,000-£1,000,
£2,400-£800 and £1,500-£500(x3)]
[op 5/2 tchd 7/2 in places] **11/4J**

4   2 **APPELLATION** (7) 2 9-0 .M Roberts
(R Hannon) *dwelt, soon tracking leaders, ridden 2f out, stayed on*
inside final furlong   [op 8/1 tchd 14/1 in a place] **12/1**

5   ½ **FAITHFUL WARRIOR (USA)** (6) 2 9-0 . . . . .J Reid
(B W Hills) *tracked leaders, ridden 2f out, one pace approaching*
last [bets of £3,000-£1,000(x3), £1,500-£500, £11,000-£4,000,
£1,100-£400 and including office money]
[op 5/2 tchd 100/30 in places] **11/4J**

6   1¼ **LONER** (10) 2 9-0 . . . . .S Whitworth
(N A Callaghan) *held up, ridden over 2f out, stayed on one pace*
from over 1f out, never near to challenge
[op 16/1 tchd 25/1 in places] **20/1**

7   shd **ROXANNE MILL** (11) 2 8-4 . . . . .G Baker(5)
(M D I Usher) *held up, ridden 2f out, some progress from over*
1f out, never nearer   [op 16/1 tchd 33/1] **20/1**

8   1¼ **MADRASEE** (4) 2 8-9 .D Sweeney
(M Blanshard) *tracked leaders, ridden 2f out, beaten approaching*
final furlong   [op 14/1 tchd 20/1 in a place] **16/1**

Figure 32(b)

9   *2* HOT PANTS (5) 2 8-2 . . . . .C Catlin(7)
       (K T Ivory) *pressed leaders, ridden over 2f out, weakened*
       entering final furlong   [op 8/1 tchd 12/1 in places] **10/1**

10   *6* BATCHWORTH LOCK (13) 2 8-11 . . . . .S Carson(3)
       (E A Wheeler) *chased leaders until faded halfway*
                                         [tchd 50/1 in places] **33/1**

11   *nk* MISS DAMINA (15) 2 8-9 . . . . .R French
       (J Pearce) *soon behind*   [op 25/1] **33/1**

12   *1¼* BRAVURA (9) 2 8-9 . . . . .I Mongan(5)
       (G L Moore) *dwelt, always behind*   [op 25/1] **33/1**

13   *hd* LEGGIT (IRE) (12) 2 8-9 t . . . . .R Havlin
       (M R Channon) *started slowly, always behind*   [op 12/1] **20/1**

14   *½* OPERATION ENVY (14) 2 9-0 . . . .(52) C Rutter
       (R M Flower) *soon outpaced*   [tchd 66/1 in a place] **50/1**

15   *2½* PACKIN EM IN (3) 2 9-0 . . . . .S Sanders
       (N Hamilton) *mid-division, ridden over 2f out, fading when veered*
       right over 1f out   **33/1**

16   *16* ATEMME (2) 2 8-9 . . . . .B Marcus
       (Miss Jacqueline S Doyle) *very slowly away, always well behind*
                                         [tchd 25/1 in a place] **20/1**

16 ran   **TIME** 58.90s (slow by 3.30s)   **SP TOTAL PERCENT** 135
1st OWNER: Joe L Allbritton BRED: Yeomanstown Stud
TRAINER: B J Mehan at Upper Lambourn, Berks
2nd OWNER: R Carstairs
3rd OWNER: Highclere Thoroughbred Racing Ltd
TOTE WIN £10.30; PL £3.40, £2.80, £2.20; EX £44.40; CSF £42.64
TRIFECTA Not won. Pool of £284.83 c/f to Wednesday.

Figure 32(c)

In this often crucial business of determining which horse is
actually causing bookmakers to revise their initial estimate of
a runner's chance, a calculator becomes necessary because, on
occasion, one has the tricky task of deciding whether the
most 'trimmed ' runner is, say, a 6–4 favourite shortening to
11–8, or a 7–2 shot falling to 3–1.

In the former example (as in all calculations that involve
different digits featuring on the right-hand sides of the two

rates of odds in question) one has first to find a common denominator for these. For the 4 and the 8 in the odds of 6–4 and 11–8 this is obviously 8. Thus, it could be said that 12/8ths (6–4) had contracted to 11/8ths – a reduction of one twelfth or, as your calculator will reveal, of 8.5 per cent. In the case of 7–2 contracting to 3–1, this is seven 'halves' contracting to six – a reduction of one seventh or of 14.28 per cent. Thus, the latter contraction emerges as the greater, and possibly the more significant. Indeed, it is often profitable if the backer can, by such pocket calculator-assisted computations, determine which horse in a race has actually attracted the heaviest 'proportional' monetary support.

CHAPTER 4

CALCULATING WHICH OUTSIDERS TO SUPPORT

In the wake of the stock market crash of 1987, the great hurricane of the same year and the San Francisco earthquake a year later, came a renewed interest in the catastrophe theory that was fist formulated in 1965 by the distinguished French mathematician, René Thom. Since Thom's theory of chaos is mathematical in nature it would seem sensible to use a pocket calculator's capacity to process numerical variables in a brave attempt to bring order into the chaos that racing can seem to represent when the results of races suddenly feature a high incidence of successful outsiders.

Catastrophe theorists might well attribute such sudden alterations from the equine behaviour that expert judges, bookmakers and the majority of backers expect to transpire to radical changes in the influences that often govern this behaviour. One of these is having a fair chance by virtue of being unburdened by any extra, previously unforeseen, 'handicap' to one's chosen horse that is imposed just before the race takes place. A particular position in the draw over a certain distance on a particular course where past results show this to be a crucial determinant is such a rogue factor in racehorse selection. In fact, sometimes to an extent greater than that produced by unsuitable going, an unfavourable draw can prevent a horse from running up to its best past form.

In essence, the search for outsiders and, by implication, value in a betting environment dominated by cramped prices against runners with readily discernible claims is an extremely sensible proceeding. Indeed, widely respected systems expert, Nick Mordin, has often stressed how profitable some winners can prove since their selection stems from contrary, intelligently divergent, thinking that differs radically from that of most backers.

As it happens, one daily newspaper – the *Daily Express* – presents the results of exhaustive research designed to pinpoint the daily races in which outsiders have the best past records. If readers find that any of these races is also an event which this paper sees as involving a marked draw bias, yet another method of racehorse selection by pocket calculator can be operated.

For example, on Tuesday 18 July 2000, the *Daily Express* – in the 'Analyser' section of its racing page – pinpointed two races as having the best past records for outsiders. These were the 3.15 at Beverley and the 4.00 at Brighton.

ANALYSER

TRAINERS (last 10 days)
C Mann 80% (1 win and 3 places from 5 runners), H Candy 71% (2/3/7), G McCourt 50% (3/0/6), M Usher 42% (2/3/12),
J Glover, on the other hand, has gone 37 runners without a win.

JOCKEYS
D Holland 36% (4 wins from 11 rides), Iona Wands 33% (4/12), D MacGaffin 25% (2/8),
G Faulkner 25% (2/8),
J P Spencer 24% (7/29). A Macaky has got his 100 up in consecutive losing rides.

Best Races For Favourites:
BEV 2.45: 70%, 2.15: 65%.

Best Races For Outsiders:
BEV 3.15: 57%, BRI 4.00: 43%.

Best Races For Trainers:
BRI 3.00: R Hannon (4 in 9 years).

Best Races For Jockeys:
BEV 2.15: J Carroll (3 winners in last 9 years).

3.15–STRUTHERS & CARTER HANDICAP
£3,302 (F)   5f   (20)

301 (10) 412154 **BOWLERS BOY (7) (C&D)** J J Quinn (7) 7 10 0 . . . . .**K Darley** 48
302 (18) 001860 **POLAR MIST (25) (D,F)** M Wigham (5) 5 9 13 . . . .**D McKeown** 42
303 (8) 0-04836 **THORNCLIFF FOX (19)** J Glover (50) 9 12 . . . .**O Pears** 44
304 (11) 550165 **LIZZIE SIMMONDS (12) (D)** N Tinkler (3) 3 9 11 **Iona Wands (5)** 42
305 (17) 036252 **GARNOCK VALLEY (8) (D)** A Berry (3) 10 9 10 . . . . .**F Lynch** 46
306 (19) 764-016 **DANCE LITTLE LADY (20) (S)** M W Easterby (4) 3 9 9 **G Parkin** 43
307 (6) 016080 **PRESS AHEAD (22)** S Bowring (35) 5 9 9 . . . .**D Gibson** 43
308 (14) 186744 **OFF HIRE (26) (D)** C Smith (27) 4 9 9 . . . .**R FitzPatrick(3)** 44
309 (13) 0-30077 ● **EASTERN PROPHETS (14) (C&D)** M Dods (2) 5 9 6
                                                                        A Culhane 45
310 (7) 600-80 **DUNKELLIN HOUSE (67)** R Fahey (2) 3 9 8 . . . . . .**P Fessey** 42
311 (5) 169500 **SOUNDS LUCKY (13) (D)** N Littmoden (17) 4 9 7 . .**D Sweeney** 47
312 (3) 05400 **GOING HOME (295)** M W Easterby (4) 3 9 7 . . . .**T Lucas** 45
313 (9) 101390- **L A TOUCH (346)** C Dwyer (6) 7 9 7 . . . .**D Mernagh(3)** 39
314 (1) 074900 **SEAHORSE BOY (6)** J Wainwright (14) 3 9 6 . . . .**T McLaughlin** 38
315 (15) 0-90709 **AMERICAN COUSIN (30) (D)** D Nicholls (2) 5 9 6
                                                                    Alex Greaves 44
316 (4) 0-67210 **DAZZLING QUINTET (9) (C&D)** C Smith (27) 4 9 6
                                                                    J McAuley(5) 47
317 (16) 329170 **INDIAN BAZAAR (8) (C&D,T)** J Bradley (4) 4 9 5 . . .**G Baker(7)** 42
318 (12) 044572 **SEALED BY FATE (3) (D)** J Wainwright (14) 5 9 5 . . .**D Holland** 44
319 (20) 004048 **DOMINELLE (9) (C&D)** T Easterby (2) 8 9 4 . . . .**J Carroll★**49
320 (2) 1-88170 **SERGEANT SLIPPER (9) (D)** C Smith (27) 3 9 2 **K Dalgleish(5)** 48

BLINKERS: Nos. 2, 20 VISOR: Nos. 3, 7, 8, 9, 18 TONGUE STRAP: No. 2.

Express Betting Forecast: — 6 Dominelle, 7 Dance Little Lady, American Cousin,
8 Bowlers Boy, Garnock Valley, Indian Bazaar, 10 Polar Mist, 12 others
1999: Bollin Ann (18) 4-9-6 J Fortune 11-2 (T Easterby) 20 ran.

GUIDE: DOMINELLE has not won for a couple of years, but as a consequence has slipped to a mark 19lb lower than when last successful and does seem to reserve her best for this course. Veteran sprinter **Garnock Valley** holds his form well and comes here on the back of a short head scored second to Branston Lucy at Musselburgh (third home has since won). **Dance Little Lady** is just 3lb higher than when scoring at Redcar and remains well treated. So does **Eastern Prophets,** who is inconsistent and has failed to score in two years. **American Cousin** is better than his form figures suggest and has dropped to a rating 3lb lower than when last successful; watch the market. **Indian Bazaar** took advantage of a favourable draw to score over C&D in June. He again has a decent berth and must be considered with his stable in form. *DRAW BIAS: High.*   JR

Figure 33(a)

4.00–JOE BLANKS CHALLENGE CUP (HCP)
£3,835 (D)   1m   (10)

1 (4) 404 ● **COPPLESTONE (14)** P Harris 4 9 10 .**Carol Packer(7)**
2 (10) 160 **DOLPHINELLE (7) (C)** J R Poulton 4 9 2 . . . . . .**O Urbina**
3 (8) 010 **FUEGIAN (15) (D)** M Madgwick 5 8 11 . . . .**M Fenton**
4 (9) 483 **MUTABASSIR (16) (C&D)** G L Moore 6 8 11 .**I Mongan(5)**
5 (7) 161 **AGIOTAGE (15) (D,S)** S C Williams 4 8 9 . . . . . .**G Carter**
6 (5) 111 **TAPAGE (34) (D)** A Reid 4 8 7 . . . .**M Henry**
7 (6) 0-67 **CEDAR LORD (75)** R O'Sullivan 3 8 2 . . . .**N Pollard**
8 (1) 1-07 **DUSKY VIRGIN (46) (C)** S Woodman 3 7 13
                    A Nicholls(3)
9 (2) 546 **LAGO DI LEVICO (29) (D)** Derrick Morris 3 7 12 . . .**P Doe**
10 (3) 80-6 **FORT KNOX (J110) (C,D)** J R Poulton 9 7 10 . . . .**A Daly**
    BLINKERS: No. 10 VISOR: No. 3.

W-Factor: Copplestone (66); Mutabassir (65); Tapage (65); Dusky Virgin (65); Lago Di Levico (65); Agiotage (64).

Express Betting Forecast: — 9–4 Tapage, 4 Agiotage, 9–2 Mutabassir, 7 Fuegian, 8 Copplestone, Dophinelle, 12 others.

1999: Khibrah (9) 3-9-0 R Hills 4-1 fav (E Dunlop) 9 ran.

Figure 33(b)

As it turned out, the latter contest was of no interest because the course details for the Brighton track given in the *Daily Express* showed that over its mile length it would confer no advantage to runners starting from particular stalls positions.

BRIGHTON

DRAW DATA: Left handed. In sprints, those drawn low are favoured, but only if they have early speed and can act on the track. Stalls Today: Inside, Except 1m3f & 1m4f – Outside.

BEVERLEY

DRAW DATA: Right handed. High numbers have a big advantage on the slightly dog-legged 5f straight course, and on the round course up to 1m1f, especially in largefields. When the going is soft, low numbers are best. Stalls Today: All Races Inside. **LONGEST TRAVELLER: White Sands** (4.45), C Cyzer, Horsham—233 miles.

Figure 34

In the 3.15 at Beverley, however, a draw bias to highly drawn runners was indicated in the *Daily Express* and elaborated upon in the information this paper provided on this Yorkshire course to the effect that 'high numbers have a big advantage over the slightly dog-legged 5f straight course' – precisely that on which the contestants for the 3.15 were due to race!

Having found the race to 'compute', the next step involved writing down the names of all runners in this that were unquoted in the *Daily Express* betting forecast. As readers may care to check, this list worked out as follows: Thorncliff Fox, Lizzie Simmonds, Press Ahead, Off Hire, Eastern Prophets, Dunkellin House, Sounds Lucky, Going Home, L.A. Touch, Seahorse Boy, Dazzling Quintet, Sealed by Fate and Sergeant Slipper.

As it happened, the good-to-firm ground to be found at Beverley on 18 July 2000 led to the eventual withdrawal of Sounds Lucky and Sergeant Slipper which left 11 outsiders. These were then reduced to six by eliminating the five with the lowest private handicap ratings (shown on the extreme right of the *Daily Express* race details). Thus, Lizzie Simmonds (with 42), Press Ahead (with 43), Dunkellin House (with 42), L.A. Touch (with 39) and Seahorse Boy (with 38) were all eliminated.

A table was then compiled containing five performance figures – precisely the same number of similar digits that have repeatedly been featured in the standard 16-step computational sequence that has been adopted on previous occasions in this book.

With regard to the six surviving outsiders, from top to bottom, the first column of this pre-prepared table featured the form ratings given to these runners in the race details provided by the *Daily Express*. Thus, this column started with

44 (against the name of Thorncliff Fox) and ended with 44 against Sealed By Fate.

The table's second column ranked the ten outsiders in order of their being favoured by the draw bias on Beverley's five-furlong course. Thus, Off Hire was 'top-rated' with ten points for being the best, i.e. the most highly drawn in stall 14, whereas Going Home was given 3 points for starting from stall 3, being the worst drawn of the six outsiders.

The table's third column featured the form figure attained by each outsider last time out. Thus, Thorncliff Fox was given six points for his last-time-out sixth place and Dazzling Quintet was given ten points for his 'duck's egg' of a last run.

The table's fourth column featured the number of placings in the first four each outsider had attained from the total number of outings shown in its form line.

Column five showed this total number as a separate performance figure.

For example: Thorncliff Fox firstly had a figure of one placed in the fourth column of the table and then six was entered in its fifth column.

For ease of reference and to facilitate both comprehension and checking, the following is the complete table of these five performance figures for all six outsiders that was prepared prior to the feeding in of these figures into the calculator according to the 16-step 'standard' procedure.

Name of Outsider	Col. 1	Col. 2	Col. 3	Col. 4	Col. 5
THORNCLIFF FOX	44	7	6	2	6
OFF HIRE	44	10	4	3	6
EASTERN PROPHETS	45	9	7	1	6
GOING HOME	45	5	10	1	5
DAZZLING QUINTET	47	6	10	2	6
SEALED BY FATE	44	8	2	1	6

Figure 35

As readers may care to check, the standard button-pressing procedure involving these table figures meant that, in table order, these outsiders were given respective final ratings of 38.73, 50.00, 27.99, 28.28, 37.86 and 28.87. This meant that Off Hire was clear top-rated to win his Beverley race which he duly did, most gratifyingly, at 16–1!

3.15 (5f Hcap) — **OFF HIRE** (R FitzPatrick) **16–1** 1; **Polar Mist 16–1** 2; **Lizzie Simmonds 14–1** 3; **Eastern Prophets 14–1** 4, **17 ran.** 4–1 Fav Dominelle (C Smith), hd, ½ nk. **Tote:** £28.60; £3.80, £5.20, £4.60, £2.20. Ex: £500.80. CSF: £243.11. Trifecta not won. Tricast: £3,484.70. NRs: Bowlers Boy, Sounds Lucky, Sergeant Slipper.

Figure 36

CHAPTER 5

CALCULATING WHICH TRAINERS' HORSES TO SUPPORT

A s one who has regularly studied the results of particular races over an extensive period, I cannot agree with Henry Ford's assertion that 'history is bunk'. In fact, the belief that on the turf the opposite is true has led Britain's racing daily, the *Racing Post*, to employ journalist Craig Thake to delve into the form books so that he can give readers some potentially profitable history lessons that result from his extremely thorough research.

As it happens, another daily newspaper goes back even further into the past in its search for significant trainer trends as regards every race on the daily cards (unlike Thake, who only deals with prestigious events). This paper is the *Daily Mail* whose 'Trainerform' statistics form part of a composite feature called 'Ahead of the Game'. Interestingly, on Thursday 13 July 2000, the paper showed that at that day's five meetings, significant trainer trends had been discovered at only one of these – Newmarket's important July meeting.

On this day, as on any other race day, the problem, as with any method of racehorse selection that throws up several qualifiers, is how to differentiate between them. In fact, on 13 July 2000, five horses were indicated as worthy of the close attention of all those who are wisely convinced that previously successful handlers often seek to replicate their past successes in particular races. As can be seen from the illustration below, the four trainers pinpointed on this particular day were H. Cecil sending out Vacamonte in Newmarket's 2.05 and Cloud Hopping in the 4.10; L. Cumani who was running East Cape in the 2.35; J. Dunlop who was responsible for eventual non-runner Red N'Socks and J. Gosden sending out Shair in the 4.10.

TRAINER FORM

GUIDE showing significant trainer trends.
NEWMARKET: H Cecil won the 2.05 in 1986, 1988, 1989, 1990, 1992, 1993, 1995 and 1997. **L Cumani** won the 2.35 in 1994 and 1997. **J Dunlop** won the 2.35 in 1987 and 1993. **H Cecil** won the 4.10 in 1989, 1992, 1993 and 1997. **J Gosden** won the 4.10 in 1994 and 1996.

NEWMARKET

FIVE-YEAR-RECORD

Jockeys: Pat Eddery 47, R Hills 35, M HIlls 31, T Quinn 26, J Reid 19, W Ryan 16, Dane O'neill 14, M Roberts 14.

Trainers: J Gosden 35, H Cecil 33, J Dunlop 31, R Hannon 29, L Cumani 23, B Hanbury 20, B Hills 18, Sir M Stoute 18.

PRINCIPAL MEETING. R-H July course. GOING: Good. STALLS: Far side; except 4.10 stands side. DRAW ADVANTAGE: None. SIS meeting. JACKPOT: All six races.

ROBIN GOODFELLOW	GIMCRACK
2.05 Vacamonte	2.05 Bonnard
2.35 Red N' Socks	2.35 Sir Ferbet
3.05 Bertolini	3.05 Pipalong
3.40 Tayseer	3.40 NICE ONE CLARE (nap)
4.10 Royal Tryst	4.10 Cloud Hopping
4.45 Seven Sing	4.45 Seven Sing

NEWMARKET (David Milnes) – 2.05 Earl Grey; 2.35 RESOUNDING (napP; 3.05 Lioncoln Dancer; 3.40 Nice One Clare; 4.10 White House.
NORTHERNER – 2.35 Adamas; 3.05 Pipalong; 3.40 Peartree House; 4.10 Biggles.

BLINKERED (VISORED OR TONGUE STRAPPED) FIRST TIME: 3.05 Monashee Mountain, Rossini.

Figure 37(a)

2.05 –WEATHERBY'S SUPERLATIVE STAKES (LISTED RACE) (CLASS A) (2-Y-O) C4 [Formcast] ▼
£20,000 added (£12,818) 7f (8)

101	(3)	1 BONNARD 43 (S) A P O'Brien(Ire) 9-0	G Duffield	77
102	(1)	14 EARL GREY 23 (S) W Jarvis 9-0	M Tebbut	●78
103	(5)	21 KING'S IRONBRIDGE 12 (C&D)(G) R Hannon 9-0	Dane O'Neill	72
104	(7)	021 MUJALINA 10 (D) E J O'Neill 9-0	M Fenton	62
105	(2)	165228 STREGONE 23 (G) B Meehan 9-0	G Mosse	77
106	(6)	3 GRYFFINDOR 12 B Meehan 8-11	Pat Eddery	62
107	(4)	47 SHADOWLESS 23 C Brittain 8-11	P Robinson	76
108	(8)	VACAMONTE H Cecil 8-11	T Quinn	–

Probable SP: 2 Vacamonte, 5–2 Bonnard, 5 King's Ironbridge, 8 Gryffindor, 10 Earl Grey, Stregone, 14 Shadowless   **FAVOURITES: 1 1 2 2 0 1 0 1 1 1**

Racemail form
Bonnard was all out to land odds of 1–2 at Fairyhouse (6f) but showed plenty of spirit and is well entered up. **Vacamonte** is a beautifully bred colt by Caerleon and out of Irish Oaks winner Wemyss Bight, but he blotted his copybook a bit when refusing to enter the stalls at Royal Ascot. **King's Ironbridge** won impressively over course and distance last time, beating 3rd placed **Gryffindor** by 4½l, and is in the Middle Park Stakes. **Earl Grey** was 2l 4th to Cd Europe in the Coventry Stakes (6f) and should again hold **Shadowless** (7th) and **Stregone** (8th).

2.35 –MONDI PACKAGING HANDICAP (CLASS C) (3-Y-O) £10,000 added (£7,709) 1m (16) C4

201	(7)	31-6309 KINGSDON 21 (T) (S) R Hannon 9-7	Dane O'Neill	74
202	(1)	3-73106 TUMBLEWEED TOR 11 (D) (S) B Meehan 9-6	G Mosse	75
203	(11)	517-207 RED N' SOCKS 21 (D) (G) J Dunlop 9-5	T Quinn	76
204	(12)	13-3000 DESERT FURY 26 (G) B Hanbury 9-5	J Mackay (5)	75
205	(13)	4-531 MOSSY MOOR 22 (D) Mrs A J Perrett 9-4	Pat Eddery	74
206	(9)	3-21071 SIR FERBET 32 (D2) (G) B Hills 9-2	M Hills	74
207	(10)	2-741 ADAMAS 16 (D) (G) A Turnell 9-1	K Darley	75
208	(5)	L-40D89 CLEVER GIRL 6 (D) (S) T Easterby 9-1	J Fortune	73
209	(16)	1L20 LOCHARATI 26 (S) J Eustace 9-0	J Tate	72
210	(3)	055-707 IYAVAYA 19 (GS) M Channon 9-0	W Supple	71
211	(14)	441-805 SPIN A YARN 32 B Hills 8-10	J Reid	76
212	(15)	51-3 RESOUNDING 31 (S) A Stewart 8-8	M Roberts	75
213	(2)	L421 EAST CAPE 17 (D) (G) L Cumani 8-8	J P Spencer	73
214	(8)	L77203 CHAPEL ROYALE 5 (D) K Mahdi 8-7	G Duffield	●78
215	(4)	221270- PHOEBE BUFFAY 272 (C Allen 8-6	D O'Donohue	71
216	(6)	14-0175 SOVEREIGN STATE 12 (D2) (GS) M Jarvis 8-5	P Robinson	72

Probable SP: 6 Sir Ferbet, 7 Spin A Yarn, 15–2 Mossy Moor, 8 Red N' Socks, East Cape, 10 Kingsdon, Resounding, 12 Tumbleweed Tor, Clever Girl.

FAVOURITES: 0 0 1 0 0 2 1 3 0 3

1999: Calcutta 3 9 0 (M Hills) 15–2 B HIlls drawn (10) 15 ran.

Sir Ferbet won a similar race on the Rowley Mile last month with **Spin A Yarn** (5lb better off) 3½l 5th. **Red N' Socks** (7th) was marginally in front of **Kingsdon** (9th) in the 32-runner Britannia Handicap (1m) at Royal Ascot. **Mossy Moor** made a winning start in handicap company at Kempton (1m) but is 6lb higher in this more competitive event. **East Cape** only beat Eve by a neck at Windsor (1m) but he had to come round the entire field to do so and would have been an unlucky loser. **Tumbleweed Tor** may need to drop a few pounds to make his mark, while **Adamas** didn't achieve a lot when winning at Beverley (1m).

Figure 37(b)

3.05 –DARLEY JULY CUP (SHOWCASE RACE) (GROUP 1) (CLASS A) £165,000 added (£95,700) 6f (11)   C4

301 (6)   1112-32 **AGNES WORLD** 23 **(D5) (GS)** H Mori(Jpn) 5-9-5 . . . . .Y Take   77
302 (1)   3320-23 **BERTOLINI** 23 **(V) (C&DC) (G)** Saeed bin Suroor 4-9-5 . . . .R Hills   77
303 (2)   124-613 **LEND A HAND** 21 **(D2BF) (GS)** Saeed bin Suroor 5-9-5 . . .J Reid ●78
304 (8)   6262-3L **MUNJIZ** 110 **(C&DD) (S)** B Hills 4-9-5 . . . . .W Supple   70
305 (5)   1-11210 **PIPALONG** 21 **(D5) (S)** T Easterby 4-9-2 . . . . .K Darley   74
306 (10) 310-401 **LINCOLN DANCER** 47 **(D2) (S)** M Jarvis 3-8-13 . . . . . .M Roberts   75
307 (3)   11-1150 **MONASHEE MOUNTAIN** 22 **(V) (DBF2) (S)** A P O'Brien(Ire)
            . . . . .3-8-13 G Duffield   72
308 (9)   1111-76 **PRIMO VALENTINO** 41 **(C&DD4BF) (GS)** P Harris 3-8-13
             . . . . .Pat Eddery   70
309 (7)   112-430 **ROSSINI** 21 **(V) (D2) (GS)** A P O'Brien(Ire) 3-8-13 . . .Paul Scallan   68
310 (4)   073404 **TRINCULO** 12 **(D)** N Littmoden 3-8-13 . . . . .J Quinn   61
311 (11) d-30239 **WINNING VENTURE** 12 **(S)** S Woods 3-8-13 . . . . .K Take   62

    Probable SP: 3 Agnes World, 7–2 Lend A Hand, 6 Bertolini, Lincoln Dancer, 7 Primo Valentino, Monashee Mountain, 9 Pipalong, 20 Rossini, 25 Munjiz.

    FAVOURITES: 0 3 0 0 2 1 2 0 1 3   **AGES:** 3 3 5 4 3 4 4 3 4 3
1999: Stravinsky 3 8 13 (M J Kinane) 8–1 A P O'Brien(Ire) drawn (6) 17 ran.

Bertolini finished 3rd to Stravinsky in a better renewal of this race last year but was ¾l behind **Agnes World** (who is 3lb better off here) when 3rd in the King's Stand Stakes (5f) last month. Even allowing for the dreadful ride that **Lend A Hand** was given in the Cork And Orrey (6f) last time, his 3l 3rd to Superior Premium there (with a below par **Pipalong** miles behind) was disappointing. The lightning quick **Primo Valentino** won last year's Middle Park Stakes over course and distance but has a disappointing recent run in Germany to overcome. **Monashee Mountain** was never sighted in the Jersey Stakes (7f) or French 2,000 Guineas (1m) and may be better at this trip but **Lincoln Dancer** would be happier on really soft ground.

Figure 37(c)

3.40 –LADBROKE BUNBURY CUP (HANDICAP) C4
(CLASS B) £40,000 added (£26,000) 7f (20)

401	(10)	2353-20 **EXEAT 22 (V)** J Gosden 4-9-12	J Fortune	72
402	(13)	11-35 **TILLERMAN 22 (CBF2) (S)** Mrs A J Perrett 4-9-12	Pat Eddery	73
403	(18)	50-83-13 **PERSIANO 22 (D3) (GS)** J Fanshawe 5-9-5	D Harrison	74
404	(15)	17-9782 **JUNO MARLOWE 20 (C&DD) (G)** P Harris 4-9-4	T Quinn	75
405	(19)	21-1223 **STRAHAN 20 (BF) (S)** J Gosden 3-9-2	K Darley	●78
406	(16)	510-0L0 **TAYIF 20 (D2) (GS)** J W Payne 4-9-1	A McGlone	75
407	(12)	3106-00 **OMAHA CITY 22 (D2) (GS)** B Gubby 6-9-1	J Reid	74
408	(11)	L-96497 **DEBBIE'S WARNING 4 (G)** K Mahdi 4-9-0	Dane O'Neill	77
409	(3)	04L/041 **CHOTO MATE 26 (D) (G)** R Hannon 4-8-13	P Dobbs (5)	77
410	(20)	13211-5 **NICE ONE CLARE 20 (C&DD2) (G)** J W Payne 4-8-12	J P Spencer	77
411	(7)	031244 **PEARTREE HOUSE 11 (DBF2) (GS)** D Nicholls 6-8-11	A Nicholls (3)	77
412	(8)	005303 **TAYSEER 12 (CD2) (GS)** D Nicholls 6-8-9	G Mosse	76
413	(2)	7050-01 **KINAN (5lbex) 8 (D) (S)** G Bravery 4-8-9	M Hills	77
414	(5)	500137 **GIFT OF GOLD 19 (D4) (GS)** A Bailey 5-8-7	G Duffield	77
415	(17)	7158-14 **A TOUCH OF FROST 26 (B) (D4) (GS)** G Margarson 5-8-6	M Fenton	74
416	(6)	150012 **SECOND WIND 13 (T) (DC&DD3) (GS)** C Dwyer 5-8-6	J Mackay (5)	76
417	(14)	401830 **PIPS SONG 20 (S)** Dr J Scargill 5-8-6	J Lowe	77
418	(4)	40/0451 **THUNDER SKY 13 (V) (D) (G)** C Brittain 4-8-3	P Robinson	75
419	(9)	91L-000 **POLES APART 27 (G)** M Tompkins 4-8-3	J Quinn	73
420	(1)	300054 **SALTY JACK 18 (D6BF) (GS)** V Soane 6-8-2	J F Egan	77

Probable SP: 5 Tillerman, 11–2 Strahan, Nice One Clare, 7 Tayseer, Persiano, 16 Peartree House, Kinan, Juno Marlowe, Salty Jack, 18 Second Wind, 20 Exeat, Choto Mate, 25 A Touch Of Frost, 28 Omaha City, Gift Of Gold, Tayif.

FAVOURITES: 2 0 0 0 0 0 2 0 0 1 (W9-2). **AGES: 4 3 4 5 6 3 4 4 3 4**
1999: Grangeville 4 9 3 (K Fallon) 13–2 JtFav I Balding drawn (20) 19 ran.

Persiano was only beaten ¾l by Caribbean Monarch (easy winner again since) in the Royal Hunt Cup (1m), and, given that he was poorly drawn there, he could well confirm his superiority over **Tillerman** (1lb better off) who was under ½l away in 5th (**Debbie's Warning** 9th, **Omaha City** 10th and **Exeat** 11th of 32). **Strahan** was a big gamble in the Wokingham (6f) and finished 2¼l 3rd to Harmonic Way, 1¾l ahead of 5th placed **Nice One Clare** (1lb better off) who was making her seasonal debut (**Pips Song** 17th of 29). **Peartree House** has been admirably consistent recently and is not necessarily David Nicholls' second string behind **Tayseer**. Although the latter did hint that a return to form may not be far away at Newcastle (7f) last time. **Second Wind** (2nd over 10f since) beat **Juno Marlowe** (7lb better off) by 3¾l, over course and distance last month with subsequent winner **Kinan** well adrift.

Figure 37(d)

4.10 –BEDFORD LODGE HOTEL MAIDEN STAKES (CLASS D)
(3-Y-O) £8,000 added (£5,655) 1m 2f (9)

501	(9)	4 BIGGLES 22 A Turnell 9-0	....	K Darley	64
502	(2)	CLOUD HOPPING H Cecil 9-0	....	T Quinn	–
503	(8)	3- KARAJAN 272 J Hills 9-0	....	M Hills	●78
504	(1)	ROYAL TRYST Sir M Stoute 9-0	....	Pat Eddery	–
505	(3)	SHAIR J Gosden 9-0	....	J Fortune	–
506	(4)	ELLWAY QUEEN B Hanbury 8-9	....	J Reid	–
507	(7)	INAAQ Saeed bin Suroor 8-9	....	R Hills	–
508	(5)	ROSE ADAGIO H Cecil 8-9	....	W Ryan	–
509	(6)	0-44 WHITE HOUSE 63 W Jarvis 8-9	....	M Tebbut	69

Probable SP: 2 Inaaq, 7–2 Cloud Hopping, Royal Tryst, 7 Rose Adagio, 8 Karajan, Shair, 14 Ellway Queen, 25 White House, 50 Biggles.
FAVOURITES: 1 0 1 0 2 1 0 1 2 0
1999: Dane 3 8 9 (M Roberts) 20–1 A Stewart drawn (5) 6 ran.
Karajan looks best of the experienced runners on his ½l 3rd to Pawn Broker over 1m here last year as **Biggles** and **White House** have not impressed in low grade maidens. The newcomers could well dominate this, however, and the Lammtarra filly **Inaaq** is in the Yorkshire Oaks. Henry Cecil's Mr Prospector colt **Cloud Hopping** and Sadler's Wells filly **Rose Adagio** are sure to be popular along with Sir Michael Stoute's Kingmambo colt **Royal Tryst** and the Warning gelding **Shair**.

4.45 – PRINCESS MAIDEN FILLIES' STAKES (CLASS D)
(2-Y-O) £8,000 added (£5,785) 6f (9)

601	(8)	U AILINCALA 13 C Wall 8-11	....	M Tebbutt
602	(3)	BENEVOLENCE S Woods 8-11	....	J Reid
603	(6)	2 ECSTATIC 45 R Hannon 8-11	....	Dane O'Neill
604	(4)	KHULAN J Dunlop 8-11	....	R Hills
605	(2)	LADY MILETRIAN M Channon 8-11	....	M Roberts
606	(7)	MUJADO B Meehan 8-11	....	Pat Eddery
607	(9)	0 RICHENDA 28 R Hannon 8-11	....	G Duffield
608	(5)	SAUCE TARTAR N Callaghan 8-11	....	K Darley
609	(1)	SEVEN SING B Hills 8-11	....	M Hills

Probable SP: 7–4 Khulan, 3 Seven Sing, 5 Ecstatic, 6 Lady Miletrian, 7 Mujado, 12 Benevolence, Sauce Tartar, 16 Richenda, 25 Ailincala.
FAVOURITES: 1 0 1 1 1 1 2 1 1 1
1999: Journalist 2 8 11 (M Hills) 13–8 Fav B Hills drawn (8) 10 ran.
Ecstatic was a neck 2nd to Gold Air on heavy ground at Sandown (5f) and represents Richard Hannon along with **Richenda**, who shaped quite well in a Newbury (6f) maiden that is working out very well. **Khulan**, by Bahri, and **Seven Sing**, a half-sister to Sussex Stakes winner Distant View, are both in the Lowther and Cheveley Park Stakes. The Barathea newcomer **Lady Miletrian** and **Mujado**, by Mujadil, are both in the former race at York next month.

(Form guide by NICK SMITH)

Figure 37(e)

The problem of how to differentiate between these qualifiers was solved by using a pocket calculator and by adopting the by now perhaps rather familiar, 16-step, button-pressing sequence which forms the cornerstone of many of the selection methods this book contains. Firstly, one gives a 'Trainer Form' qualifying horse a points score for being selected by one or more of the *Daily Mail's* regular correspondents who pick a horse for every race on the day's cards. These pundits are Robin Goodfellow, Gimcrack and Formcast, the *Mail's* private handicapper. As can be seen above, in the case of the first Trainer Form qualifier, Vacamonte, this two-year-old (for being the selection of Robin Goodfellow alone) was given a points score of 10. (Had all three *Mail* experts gone for him, he would have received a total score of 30, i.e. 3 × 10.) This figure of 10 was then entered into the calculator.

Next, after pressing the + sign, another 'performance' digit was entered. This was derived from the betting forecast and for figuring first in this Vacamonte was given 10 points. (Had he been in fourth place in this forecast, he would have received 7 points, if in third place 8 points and, if in tenth place, one point.) Thus, 10 was next entered into the calculator and its minus key pressed.

WHO'S HOT

TRAINERS (last 14 days) G Bravery 3 wins from 6 runners (50%), J Noseda 4 from 9 (44%), H Cecil 7 from 16 (44%), R Brotherton 3 from 8 (38%), A P O'Brien 7 from 20 (35%), R Charlton 5 from 15 (33%).

Figure 38

After this, 'Who's Hot', another *Daily Mail* feature on trainers' past (but this time very recent) performances was consulted to see if Vacamonte's handler was in current winning form. As Cecil was shown in 'Who's Hot' with a second place strike rate of 44 per cent, Vacamonte was given 2 points. (Had he been trained by 'top of the table' G. Bravery, he would have been given 1 point, and if by bottom-placed R. Charlton, 6 points.)

This 'Who's Hot' score of 2 was then entered into the calculator and, in exact accordance with the next stages in our 'standard' button-pressing sequence so often featured in this book, the = and × keys were next pressed. NB If the handler of a Trainer Form qualifier does not feature in 'Who's Hot', he or she should be given a points score of 10.

Then the number of Vacamonte's handler's successes in the last 10 years, also given in Trainer Form's column – i.e. five, in 1990, 1992, 1993, 1995 and 1997 – became the next 'performance related' digit to be entered into the calculator.

After entry of the = and × signs and after the figure of 100 had been entered and the ÷ sign pressed, it was time to enter the total number of times (ten) that Cecil could possibly have been successful during the previous decade. Then the = key was pressed and finally, the √ button to determine the square root of 900 which, at 30.00, became Vacamonte's final 'Trainer Form' rating.

As readers may care to check, on 13 July 2000, no other rival Trainer Form qualifier was able to surpass this score. In the event, Vacamonte ran out a very easy 7–4 winner and so earned the rave review in the following day's *Daily Mail*, shown in Figure 39.

NEWMARKET Gd to soft

2.05 (7f 2yo) — **VACAMONTE** (T Quinn **7–4 Fav** 1; **Shadowless 12–1** 2; **Bonnard 11–2** 3. 8 ran. (H Cecil). 3½, hd. **Tote:** £2.70; £1.50, £2.40, £1.50. Exacta: £31.90. CSF: £20.58. Trifecta: £97.90.

HENRY CECIL introduced a very promising two-year-old in Vacamonte who easily won the Superlative Stakes at Newmarket yesterday by three and a half lengths from Shadowless. The colt is now a 33–1 shot for the 2,000 Guineas with Corals.
'This horse would have won by five or six lengths more if the going had been fast,' Cecil said.

Figure 39

CHAPTER 6

CALCULATING WHICH JOCKEYS' MOUNTS TO SUPPORT

A s top-flight jockey Frankie Dettori once demonstrated so spectacularly by riding all seven winners at an Ascot meeting in September 1996, nothing can succeed like success when one is riding racehorses. Indeed, time after time during racing seasons some jockeys experience periods when their winning runs seem almost magically prolonged.

It is the belief that, when their confidence is high, this gives jockeys an extra 'winning edge' that underpins the rationale behind yet another pocket calculator-based method of racehorse selection. As with the previous strategy on winning trainers, this dispassionate device can allow the backer to make wise and disciplined discriminations between the claims of several 'system qualifiers' – in this case between horses due to be ridden by a jockey whose very recent past successes have come so frequently as to suggest he or she is 'on a roll'.

Fortunately, one daily newspaper's racing page indicates which jockeys are 'hot' through having gained such success. This again is the *Daily Mail* and, on Monday 16 July 2000, its 'Who's Hot' jockeys' feature read as shown in Figure 40.

WHO'S HOT

JOCKEYS G Faulkner 3 wins from 9 rides (33%), A P McCoy 3 from 10 (30%), D Holland 4 from 17 (24%), Alex Greaves 3 from 13 (23%), G Baker 6 from 27 (22%), R Havlin 5 from 25 (20%), J P Spencer 8 from 41 (20%), J Mackay 7 from 37 (19%).

Figure 40

When armed with such in-depth information, what one needs is some way of differentiating between the understandably often quite numerous horses these currently high-flying pilots are due to partner. Of such jockeys listed in the paper on the day in question, G. Faulkner, the highest-rated, was, rather surprisingly, due to ride only one horse – an untipped, 14–1 shot at rather lowly Windsor. His mount was thus ignored.

6.30 –GREAT ORMOND STREET CHILDRENS HOSPITAL E.B.F. MEDIAN AUCTION MAIDEN STAKES (CLASS E) (2-Y-O) £4,000 added (£2,951) 5f 10yds (13)

1	(12)	6	**AVERY RING 39** A Jarvis 9-0	B Marcus	77
2	(6)	0	**BATCHWORTH LOCK 39** E Wheeler 9-0	D Kinsella (7)	60
3	(10)		**MISHKA** J C Poulton 9-0	A Daly	–
4	(3)	L5	**RAMBLIN' MAN 16** V Soane 9-0	G Hind	–
5	(8)	63L2	**RUSHBY 31** Mrs P Dutfield 9-0	L Newman (3)	●78
6	(5)	332	**WESTERN HERO 7** R Hannon 9-0	Dane O'Neill	75
7	(13)		**BE MY TINKER** G Brown 8-9	M Fenton	–
8	(7)	9	**ELLENDUNE GIRL 19** D Ffrench Davis 8-9	J Mackay (5)	–
9	(2)	0	**FIRST DEGREE 21** S C Williams 8-9	G Faulkner (3)	–
10	(9)		**FLAPDOODLE** A Carroll 8-9	C Rutter	–
11	(11)		**KOMENA** J W Payne 8-9	A McGlone	–
12	(4)	36	**MADRASEE 9** M Blanshard 8-9	D Sweeney	72
13	(1)	6	**MARE OF WETWANG 7** J Bethell 8-9	R Lappin	60

Probable SP: 9–4 Rushby, 3 Western Hero, 7 Avery Ring, Mare of Wetwang, 8 Madrasee, 14 First Degree, 20 Mishka, Be My Tinker, Ellendune Girl.

Of the other 'hot' jockeys listed above, the best hope of A.P. McCoy clearly involved an unappealing 1–12 shot in the 3.30 at Newton Abbot. This too was discarded for representing poor value.

3.30–HARCOMBE NOVICES' HURDLE (CLASS E) £4,000 added (£2,659) 3m 3f (4)

1	26-2111	**ARDOUR GLOWING 16 (C) (GS)** M Pipe 6-11-13 . . . . . .**A P McCoy** ●**78**
2		**DARCY JONES** Miss D Cole 4-10-10 . . . .**Mr N Harris** –
3	5LL8-65	**NEARLY DECENT 17** J Mullins 5-10-9 . . . .**S Curran** 51
4	LFP/775	**SID'S PRETENCE 31** P Farrell 9-10-9 . . . .**J Culloty** 40

Probable SP: 1–12 Ardour Glowing, 12 Sid's Pretence, 14 Nearly Decent, 33 Darcy Jones.   **FAVOURITES: - - - - - - - - - 0**   **AGES: - - - - - - - - - 4**
1999: Watkins 4-10-3 (P Flynn) 16–1 A T Murphy 6 ran.

Figure 42

However, third-placed 'hot' jockey D. Holland, with rides in Ayr's first three races, seemed worthy of scrutiny designed to identify the one horse on which he might zoom to further success.

AYR

FIVE-YEAR-RECORD

Jockeys: K Darley 23, J Fortune 20, D Holland 19, A Culhane 14, N Kennedy 12, J F Egan 10, F Lynch 8, G Duffield 8.

Trainers: B Hills 26, M Johnston 20, Miss L Perratt 14, J Goldie 11, D Nicholls 9, A Bailey 9, Sir M Stoute 7, T Easterby 6.

PRINCIPAL MEETING. L-H course. GOING: Good to firm. STALLS: Round inside; straight stands side. DRAW ADVANTAGE: High. SIS meeting. JACKPOT: All six races.

Figure 43(a)

2.15 –E.B.F. MAIDEN STAKES (CLASS D) (2-Y-O) £5,000 added (£3,679) 6f (8)

| Formcast |

101	(7)	L	AMEN CORNER 19 M Johnston 9-0	D Holland	●78
102	(4)	64	BALL GAMES 53 D Moffatt 9-0	G Duffield	71
103	(1)		HO PANG YAU Miss L Perratt 9-0	G Carter	–
104	(2)	6	LENNEL 19 D Smith 9-0	M Roberts	63
105	(6)	38	LITTLE TASK 8 A Berry 9-0	O Pears	68
106	(3)		SHATIN PLAYBOY Miss L Perratt 9-0	K Darley	–
107	(5)	6	MILLIKEN PARK 46 Miss L Perratt 8-9	R Hills	71
108	(8)	70	THORNTOUN DANCER 66 J Goldie 8-9	Dean McKeown	58

Probable SP: 9–4 Amen Corner, 5 Milliken Park, 11–2 Lennel, 6 Ball Games, Ho Pang Yau, 7 Little Task, 10 Shatin Playboy, 16 Thorntoun Dancer.

FAVOURITES: - - - - 3 1 2 1 3 1

1999: Nicholas Dudley 9 0 (G Duffield) Evens Fav Sir M Prescott dr (7) 10 ran.

2.45 –GARRY OWEN NURSERY HANDICAP (CLASS E) (2-Y-O) £4,000 added (£2,811) 7f (7)

201	(2)	0611	TORTUGUERO 10 (C&DD) (G) B Hills 9-7	M Hills	76
202	(3)	5371	PEREGIAN 12 (D) (G) M Johnston 8-9	D Holland	●78
203	(1)	533	CARRABAN 52 B Meehan 8-8	T Quinn	70
204	(6)	633	LADY BEAR 14 R Fahey 8-2	G Duffield	77
205	(7)	L29213	CEDAR TSAR 6 (D) D Chapman 8-0	D Mernagh (3)	77
206	(4)	947	NISAN BIR 19 T Easterby 7-12	P Fessey	76
207	(5)	69727	CARTMEL PRINCE 11 D Moffatt 7-10	J Bramhill	77

Probable SP: 5–4 Tortuguero, 7–2 Peregian, 13–2 Cedar Tsar, 7 Lady Bear, Nisan Bir, 10 Carraban, 16 Cartmel Prince.

FAVOURITES: - - - - - - - 1 2 0   **(W 9-0)**

1999: Clever Girl 2 8 8 (L Charnock) 10–1 T Easterby drawn (4) 12 ran.

3.15 –ROCK STEADY 20TH ANNIVERSARY HANDICAP (CLASS E) (3-Y-O) £4,000 added (£2,974) 7f (10)

301	(5)	601924	COWBOYS AND ANGELS 18 (D) (S) W G M Turner 9-7		
				Darren Williams (5)	76
302	(1)	1-09455	INDIAN MUSIC 5 (B) (S) A Berry 9-7	G Carter	76
303	(9)	1-084L3	BAJAN BELLE 36 (G) M Johnston 9-7	D Holland	75
304	(6)	L02-863	WELCOME TO UNOS 11 M Dods 9-3	F Lynch	76
305	(4)	2665L7	MYTTON'S AGAIN 2 (B) (D) (S) A Bailey 8-11	J Fortune	77
306	(8)	522590	NOWT FLASH 8 (D) B Rothwell 8-9	M Roberts	75
307	(7)	08L773	GRANITE CITY 11 J Goldie 8-0	Kimberley Hart	●78
308	(3)	0-07784	CALLING THE SHOTS 8 (V) W Storey 8-0	J Bramhill	76
309	(10)	0-7L444	ROBIN HOOD 42 Miss L Perratt 8-0	Dale Gibson	70
310	(2)	L0-401L	PHILAGAIN 7 (G) Miss L Perratt 7-10	N Kennedy	72

Probable SP: 7–2 Cowboys and Angels, 4 Bajan Belle, Welcome To Unos, 6 Indian Music, 10 Nowt Flash, Granite City, 12 Mytton's Again.

FAVOURITES: - - - - - - - 2 0 2   **(W 8-10).**

1999: On Till Morning 3 9 2 (K Darley) 6–1 P Calver drawn (9) 18 ran.

Figure 43(b)

As can be seen from Figure 44, such scrutiny involved differentiating between the claims of Amen Corner in the 2.15, Peregian in the 2.45 and Bajan Belle in the 3.15.

ROBIN GOODFELLOW	GIMCRACK
2.15 Little Task	2.15 Amen Corner
2.45 Carraban	2.45 Peregian (nb)
3.15 Bajan Belle	3.15 Mytton's Again
3.45 Beat All	3.45 ISLAND HOUSE (nap)
4.15 Legs Be Family	4.15 Xanadu
4.45 Polar Challenge	4.45 Polar Challenge

Figure 44

The first stage in this process involved various 'performance' points for each of these runners being entered into the pocket calculator. For being the forecast favourite, Amen Corner was given 10 points – had he been the second favourite, he would have received nine.

This figure of 10 was entered into the calculator and its + sign pressed. Next Amen Corner was given 20 points (i.e. 2 × 10) for being both the selection of the *Daily Mail*'s private handicappper, Formcast, and of Gimcrack, one of its two main tipsters. Had the second of these, Robin Goodfellow, also selected this runner, it would have been given a maximum score of 30 points (3 × 10).

The calculator's – sign was then pressed and Amen Corner's jockey, D. Holland, given 3 points for being in third place in the 'Who's Hot' jockey table (above). Had Holland been in first place in this, he would have been given a 'pole position' single point and 10 points had he not been mentioned in it.

Following on from this, the calculator's = sign and its × key were pressed, and from information in the 'Who's Hot' feature the total number of Holland's recent successes (4) was then entered. After this, the calculator's = sign was pressed followed by its × sign. The figure of 100 was next entered and then the ÷ sign pressed.

Subsequently, the total number of Holland's recent rides that had yielded these four successes (i.e. 17) was entered, the = sign pressed and finally the calculator's √ button engaged to give this particular Holland-partnered runner a final rating of 25.20.

As readers may care to check, this exceeded the rating of 24.73 that Holland's other mount, Peregian, was accorded and that of 19.40 given to Bajan Belle.

Thus, Amen Corner became a confident selection and won. Other winners were, incidentally, the better-priced and second-rated Peregian and the very much 'expected', but discarded, mount of Tony McCoy, Ardour Glowing, which added to his earlier success in Newton Abbot's first race.

AYR   Good to firm

2.15 (6f 2yo) – **AMEN CORNER** (D Holland) **4–6 Fav** 1; **Little Task** (O Pears) **12–1** 2; **Lennel** (M Roberts) **10–1** 3. **7 ran.** (M Johnston, Middleham). 2, nk. **Tote:** £1.50; £1.10, £3.80. Exacta: £6.30. CSF: £7.16. Trifecta: £13.40. NR: Milliken Park. **Rule 4 applies, deduct 5p in the pound.**

2.45 (7f 2yo Hcap) – **PEREGIAN** (D Holland) **2–1 Fav** 1; **Tortuguero** (M Hills) **5–2 (2ndFav)** 2; **Cedar Tsar** (D Mernagh) **10–1** 3. **7 ran.** (M Johnston, Middleham). nk, 5. **Tote:** £2.80; £1.40, £1.50. Ex: £5.40. CSF: £5.53.

3.15 (7f Hcap) – **COWBOYS AND ANGELS** (Darren Williams) **9–4 Fav** 1; **Calling The Shots** (J Bramhill) **10–1** 2; **Philagain** (N Kennedy) **25–1** 3. **10 ran.** (W G M Turner, Sherborne). hd, 2. **Tote:** £3.90; £1.80, £4.10, £4.50. Ex: £74.90. CSF: £26.39. Trifecta: £333.60. Tricast: £433.81.

3.45 (1m 2f) – **ENDLESS HALL** (J P Spencer) **7–1** 1; **Beat All** (K Darley) **11–4 (2ndFav)** 2; **Port Vila** (R Hills) **10–3** 3. 9–4 Fav Island House. (L Cumani, Newmarket) shd, 3½. **Tote:** £8.70; £2.90, £2.10. Ex: £28.60. CSF: £24.71.

4.15 (5f Hcap) – **SHARP HAT** (A Culhane) **11–2** 1; **Xanadu** (K Dalgleish) **5–2 Fav** 2; **Facile Tigre** (J Bramhill) **25–1** 3. 8 ran. (D Chapman, York). nk, 1¼. **Tote:** £5.80; £1.60, £1.60, £4.00. Ex: £16.30. CSF: £20.67. Tf: £559.50. Tricast: £317.00. NRs: Pips Magic, Sir Sandrovitch.

4.45 (1m 2f) – **DELAMERE** (J Fortune) **9–4 (2ndFav)** 1; **Tigre** (M Hills) **11–2** 2; **Polar Challenge** (F Lynch) **8–11 Fav** 3. **5 ran.** (J Gosden, Manton). 1, hd. **Tote:** £3.80; £1.70, £2.30. Ex: £13.50. CSF: £13.82.

Jackpot: £50,056.40.

Placepot: £82.50. **Quadpot:** £59.00.

NEWTON ABBOT   Good

2.00 (2m 5f 110yds Ch) – **VENT D'AOUT** (A P McCoy) **4–9 Fav** 1; **Willows Roulette** (L Cummins) **14–1** 2; **Speedy Snaps Image** (S Burrough) **20–1** 3. **9 ran.** (M Pipe, Wellington). 20, 3½. **Tote:** £1.80; £1.20, £1.80, £2.50. Ex: £8.50. CSF: £7.91. Trifecta: £64.60. NR: Khatani.

2.30 (2m 1f Hdle) – **INTOX III** (A Duchene) **9–1** 1; **Thrashing** (J Mogford) **20–1** 2; **Ledham** (R Johnson) **10–11 Fav** 3. **13 ran.** (M Pipe, Wellington). 5 1½. **Tote:** £14.20; £3.20, £2.70, £1.10. Ex: £233.20. CSF: £145.67. Trifecta: £94.00

3.00 (3m 2f 110yds Hcap Ch) – **FREDDIE MUCK** (C Llewellyn **5–1** 1; **The Gopher** (W Marston) **5–2** 2; **Hand Woven** (A P McCoy) **9–4 (2ndFav)** 3. **4 ran.** 7–4 Fav Derring Bridge. (N Twiston-Davies, Cheltenham) 6, dist. **Tote:** £6.10; Ex: £18.10. CSF: £15.85.

3.30 (3m 3f Hdle) – **ARDOUR GLOWING** (A P McCoy) **1–16 Fav** 1; **Sid's Pretence** (J Culloty) **20–1** 2; **Nearly Decent** (S Curran) **16–1 (2ndFav)** 3. **4 ran.** (M Pipe, Wellington). 20, dist. **Tote:** £1.10. Ex: £2.20. CSF: £2.63.

4.00 (2m 110yds Hcap Ch) – **RUN FOR COVER** (C Maude) **4–1** 1; **Come On Penny** (O McPhall) **14–1** 2; **Nearly Decent** (S Curran) **16–1 (2ndFav)** 3. **8 ran.** 11–8 Fav Noble Comic. (Mrs P Dutfield, Seaton). 22, 1½. **Tote:** £4.90; £1.30, £2.70, £1.60. Ex: £32.10. CSF: £46.15. Trifecta: £151.10. Tricast: £164.09. NR: Karachi.

4.30 (2m 1f Hcap Hdle) – **AIR ATTACHE** (J Culloty) **8–1** 1; **Some Might Say** (F Keniry) **5–1 (Jt2ndFav)** 2; **Bohill Lad** (R Wakley) **11–2** 3. **7 ran.** 7–4 Fav Cage Aux Folles. (C Mann, Upper Lambourn). 12, 9. **Tote:**

Figure 45

POSTSCRIPT

By now it should be abundantly clear that the pocket calculator possesses a vast potential for finding winning racehorses that few have dreamt of or appreciated.

Currently this potential is increasing as horse racing receives ever more sophisticated quantitative coverage. Rather than the often time-consuming and tedious task of inputting data into a computer to run a programme whose rationale and precise workings remain a mystery, the racing enthusiast who takes up button-pressing on a pocket calculator has work to do that he or she is likely to find absorbingly pleasant, easy to perform and, above all, potentially profitable.

Indeed, when the results of races are seen to confirm prior calculations – as in the many examples contained in this book – one is certain to experience immense satisfaction and delight.

INDEX